The B.A.B.E.S.' G

The B.A.B.E.S.' Guide to Generational Wealth

Copyright © 2019, M. Reese Everson

All rights reserved. Except as provided by the Copyright Act of 1976 no part of this publication may be reproduced, stored in a retrieval system or transmitted in any form or by any means, electronic, mechanical, photocopying, recording, or otherwise, in either foreign or domestic language without the prior written permission of the author.

Permission to reproduce in any part must be obtained in writing from
SugarPlum Publishing
875 10th ST NW
Washington, DC 20001

Unless otherwise indicated all scripture references
are from the King James Version of the Bible.

Disclaimer: This book does not contain legal nor investing advice. If you need legal advice you should seek out a qualified attorney. If you need investing advice you should seek out a qualified financial adviser.

Cover Photo taken by: Aaron J. Thornton for Digital Depictions, LLC.
www.DigitalDepictionsLLC.com
Cover Styling by: M. Reese Everson

Table of Contents

Dedication	3
Introduction	4
Chapter 1: Wealth-Building Mindset	9
Chapter 2: Generational Wealth	16
Chapter 3: Education - The Key That Opens Doors	26
Chapter 4: Saving For Wealth	44
Chapter 5: Reverse Mortgages, Mortgages & Credit	55
Chapter 6: Real Estate	72
Chapter 7: Insurance is Your Friend	82
Chapter 8: Investing in Your Future	101
Chapter 9: EntrepreneuHERship	120
Chapter 10: Your True Inheritance	134
I want to hear from you!	144
Be a Part of the Movement!	145
Glossary: B.A.B.E.S.' Wealth-cabulary	146

Note: There are words that I will use that you may have never heard of. On the journey to building generational wealth, there is a whole new vocabulary you will have to become familiar with. If the word is in **bold** and has a tiny number next to it, I define the word in the Wealth-cabulary in the last section of the book. Be sure to check it out.

Dedication

I dedicate this book to my late grandmother, Elizabeth, who was the first Beautiful, Ambitious, Brilliant, EntrepreneuHER (B.A.B.E.) Millionaire I ever met…

To my late grandfather, Cedric, a man who spoiled me with love, showered me with affection, gifted me with knowledge, and confidence and raised me with wisdom.

I love you both for eternity.

And to all of my fellow B.A.B.E.S.: Beautiful, Ambitious, Brilliant, EntrepreneuHERs destined for Success, you are on a path to great wealth! You may not understand how to build wealth yet, but by the end of this book, you'll have plenty of ideas. Some people may not understand the correlation between God and money, but I dedicate this book to every young woman who knows that God can raise great nations from your womb only if you are willing to listen and learn. This book is dedicated to those who believe that "It's not about how you start, but how you finish."

Introduction

"Success belongs to those who believe in the power of their dreams."

Welcome back B.A.B.E.S.! First, I want to use this opportunity to express how excited I am to have you here with me again. I pray that the knowledge I will share will be a blessing to you. And if this is our first meeting, I'd like to welcome you to the sisterhood of Beautiful, Ambitious, Brilliant, EntrepreneuHERs, a group of like-minded women destined for Success. As a part of the B.A.B.E.S. community, you have joined forces with other B.A.B.E.S., for whom wealth is our birthright.

When you picked up this book, you joined me on a journey to build your life and legacy to achieve your goals. Having had past experiences of losing it all and getting it back (and then some), I'm able to share with you the tools needed to cultivate wealth and the bold steps involved. The experiences that I share in this book are the God's honest truth. When I first started writing them out in 2015, I wrote them the exact way those situations unfolded in my life: dramatic and cinematic. The first five chapters of the novel that I wrote could easily be made into a Tyler Perry movie because the situations I faced were unfathomable, unbelievable, and shocking. I had repeated instances of "OH MY GOD!" and "OH, no she didn't!" The only thing missing was the signature reality show element of a drink being thrown in someone's face, someone's wig being pulled off (likely mine), and the police being called — well, actually, that part did happen.

But then, I remembered that B.A.B.E.S. don't have time for "useless drama" in life. We don't need another ghettofabulous storyline. As B.A.B.E.S., we are known to look past failures and turn them to favor. Furthermore, if I gave you only the drama and not the education, I'd be cheating you out of all the priceless information I've learned. So, I took a step back and re-wrote this as a B.A.B.E.S.' Guide to help you learn the ins and outs of generational wealth: to give you not just the story, but the blueprint.

See, I'm not the first person to be targeted by inheritance theft. Money is quite notorious for bringing out the worst in people, particularly family. But it wasn't just the loss of my inheritance that was so unique; it was the many lessons along the way and the journey to restoration that I needed to share with you. Each step of the way, I reached a fuller understanding about life, about God, and about faith. From the very start of this journey, right after my grandmother passed, I encountered total strangers who came to randomly tell me, "Your Grandmother's house is yours." And God always confirms His Word, right? Although I wholeheartedly believed that God's words can't come back void, it was hard to keep the faith when a sheriff was doing an eviction on my grandmother's home. That prompted me to write this book — to motivate you to hold on when it seems like all is lost.

After my grandmother passed away, I learned so much about who she was as a businesswoman and more too about my grandfather as a businessman. As I cleaned out their papers and documents, I learned about their investments, business ventures and real estate holdings. I realized how enterprising they were. I knew I wanted to follow in their footsteps and carry on their legacy in a way that would make them proud of me. But why keep all of that to myself? What's success without a sisterhood of women to share it with? And based on the statistics regarding the generational wealth gap in America being larger than it was 40 years ago, it's quite clear that our community needs this information badly!

Although my journey has been a difficult one, I know that it was part of God's plan for me. I have always been intrigued by money, entrepreneurship and how wealth was built — I took a number of finance courses at Michigan State University and I worked on the Financial Services Committee for the United States House of Representatives. So I'd heard about wealth discussed in theory, but being the target of inheritance theft gave me a whole new view of how wealth is transferred and what laws governs it. I got to see the interworking of wealth and learned about estates, probate, trusts, deeds, and conveyances. To my surprise, these topics were fascinating. Knowing how to make money is one thing, but knowing how to keep it and grow it? Now that's power!

Little did I know that wealth was written into my DNA. Growing up, I had no clue that I was even a trust fund baby. I just knew that I loved the movie, "Clueless" and the idea of living in a huge Beverly Hills mansion I studied this movie and looked for clues to learn how to become wealthy. In the movie, the rich Beverly Hills socialite explains that her father was a "litigator." I had no idea what that meant, but I just knew I wanted to be one.

As time went on, I realized that I had a passion for social justice, and being an ambulance chaser would not allow me to serve others. I liked the idea of being able to earn a good living while doing good in my community, so I followed the path of education and public service. But along the way, I learned that building wealth was not the same as making money. Building wealth involves retaining and growing money through investments. Protecting wealth requires placing money in tax-deferred vehicles, and transferring wealth happens with special accounts, policies, and legal entities. Join me as I share with you the tools to secure wealth for yourself, your children and your children's children.

Mirror, Mirror...

Describe your relationship with money in one word
___

Describe your family's wealth status in two words
___

Are you proud of your relationship with money?
___

Would you say you are good with money?
___

What do you enjoy spending money on?
___

What do hate spending money on?
___

Are you happy with how much money you have?
___

How much money would you like to have?
___

How do you feel when someone gives you money?
___

What would make you a better steward of money?
___

Are you comfortable with your income?
___

Do you prefer to let men make decisions about money?
___

What do you want to spend more money on?
_____

What would you like to spend less money on?
_____

Are you proud of your credit score?
_____

Are you an investHer? What have you invested in?
_____

Who taught you about money? Investing? Credit?
_____

Who encouraged you the most to learn about money?
_____

Who discouraged you the most about your money habits?
_____

Who helps you when you need money?
_____

Are you comfortable asking to borrow money?
_____

How often are you in need of help financially?
_____

Do you have money saved for a rainy day? How much?
_____

What would you like to leave for your children? Their children?
_____

Chapter 1: *Wealth-Building Mindset*

If you read the B.A.B.E.'S Guide to Winning in the Workplace: You Don't Have to Compromise, you may recall that I shared a story in Chapter 10 about three sisters. These women, Jemima, Keziah, & Keren-happuch, were the daughters of a man named Job. Most people know the story of how Job was tested by God, how all of his children died, and how his wife told him that he should curse God and die. You may also recall how God said that even if he took everything tangible from Job, that Job's love for God would remain unchanged. Job proved God to be right and when God saw that Job loved Him for who He was and not for what He could give him, He decided to restore Job with twice as much as he had lost. Job was even blessed with a whole new family including three beautiful daughters.

Job loved his daughters so much that the Bible said he gave them an inheritance among their brothers. What is an inheritance?[1] An **inheritance** is the gift of honor and support given by a patriarch to his sons (and sometimes to his daughters). It is meant for provision and to preserve the status of the family. During that time, leaving a financial inheritance for a woman was uncommon. First, because a woman was the responsibility of her husband and was not expected to provide for herself. Second, women were often seen as the property of their husbands, it was uncommon for property to own property. Third, because women typically did not manage male-dominated issues like money and property. Typically, the inheritance was left to the males in the family who were expected to become the future husbands and providers. Yet, these three sisters were given an inheritance along with their brothers.

Nothing further was mentioned about these women who were the only women to receive a financial inheritance in the Bible. There are many Biblical stories about money, stewardship and men with birthrights, but only these three women received an actual inheritance.

Like Jemima, Keziah, and Keren-happuch, I was loved and favored by my patriarch so much so that I was gifted with the ultimate security: homeownership. Although I was one of three grandchildren and the other two were boys, I was the eldest and the apple of my grandfather's eye. My grandparents deeded the family home to me when I was only 5 years old. Yes, at 5 years of age, I became a homeowner, although I didn't have a clue of what that meant at the time. My only concern back then was if I would be able to drive my pink Barbie Jeep up and down the block after school, if Bambi's mother would be shot during the movie just like she was the other 100 times and if the ice cream truck was coming that day.

On the other hand, my grandparents in all their wisdom, were concerned that if they didn't care for me, no one else would. My parents conceived me right after their 21st birthdays, and Grandma and Papa wanted to make sure that I was well provided for. They wanted to be sure that if anything happened to them, I would have a place to call a home, especially since, according to Papa, my parents didn't have "a pot to piss in or a window to throw it out of." Also, my grandfather was a God-fearing man who took Proverbs 13:22 to heart when it said, "A good man leaveth an inheritance to his children's children."

Owning a house was a big deal for Black folk who were one generation removed from those who came up from the South during the Great Migration to start a new life working in the automotive industry. My great-grandparents settled in Detroit, the "Motor City" and had 10 children, one of them being my Papa, Cedric. After being honorably discharged from the army, Papa worked over 40 years at Chrysler Automotive in production management and was even promoted to General Foreman. Being able to own a house was a huge accomplishment for a Black man with a high school diploma and it materialized because he worked diligently to put the bricks in place to build **wealth**[2].

My grandfather decided that he wanted to build wealth early in his life. But Papa didn't just wake up one day and have what he needed to be wealthy; instead, he operated every day with a **wealth-building mentality**. Wealth existed in his mind, way before it manifested in his pockets. In addition to working a full time job as a supervisor at Chrysler, he used the money he made to purchase not just valuable possessions, but substantial **assets** that he left as his legacy. My grandfather recognized that money was a seed, and he could either eat his seed — and constantly have to go back and get more, or he could plant his seeds and wait for them to grow into a tree that would continue to produce fruit and seeds for him exponentially. While most people traded their time working for money, my grandfather learned that he could use his money to make even more money. My grandfather used his money to purchase **assets**[3] and those assets had the ability to **appreciate**[4] which increased his wealth. I call that "putting your money to work."

    My grandfather knew that putting his money to work would allow him gain freedom and power. When you can decide what you want to do with your time because you don't have to worry about trading eight hours a day just to earn enough money to stay afloat, you will have freedom and power. When you have freedom and power you can choose to build with your money and you can put a plan in place to thrive, not just survive. When you have enough money, you are free to choose the best medical care, afford the best foods, live in the best neighborhoods, send your children to the best schools, and enjoy the best that life has to offer. When my grandfather got sick, because of the wealth he has amassed, he was able to be treated by top doctors in the area and have nurses come to the house each day, to care for him without it putting a strain on my grandmother. Papa's quality of life was greatly enhanced by the assets he had purchased, including the house that he owned free and clear. He was able to live in it comfortably until he passed away.

    For a couple like my grandparents, who weren't college educated and grew up dirt-poor, building wealth was quite uncommon — particularly because assets like homeownership were beyond the reach of most Blacks at the time. President Lyndon Johnson signed the Fair Housing Act (FHA) in 1968, a landmark law passed in the aftermath of Martin Luther King, Jr.'s assassination that banned discriminatory practices in housing. In 1970, two years after the FHA passed, [Black homeownership] was 41.6 percent. My grandparents bought a plot of land on Detroit's Eastside in 1966 before the FHA was passed and had their home built from the ground up. With only 41% of Blacks even owning homes, to have a home built was remarkable. Close to 60% of Blacks at that time were still renting.

Why so few homeowners? African-Americans were categorically prevented from borrowing the money they needed to buy theirs homes due to **redlining**[5], which refused loans specifically to the black populace with the excuse that they lived in areas that were deemed to be a poor financial risk. The reality was, banks were run by people who were racist and discriminated against every Black family that came through their doors. The same racism that paid Blacks lower wages than Whites for the same work also wrote rules, legislation and policies that locked Blacks out of the mortgages needed to become homeowners.

Combining discriminatory bank lending policies with inequality in pay, one can see why blacks lagged behind in the racial wealth gap. Blacks had such a hard time building wealth and there was a substantial gap in the wealth of almost all Black families compared to almost the White families. In 1963, "the average Black family had $18,892 of wealth, while the average White family had $136,221 of wealth." Thats a $117,000 gap between the wealth of Black families and white families. Due to my grandfather's wealth building mindset, even with three children and a wife who loved to shop, he worked hard (and smart) to be able to buy land and pay for the construction of a home so that his family could stop renting.

My grandfather knew that homeownership meant not paying a landlord to rent a place to live in, but instead owning the land and structure where he lived, so that he could build equity. Having equity meant he had rights to the value of the home and land that he owned. Equity allowed him to grow his wealth without restraints. The more valuable the property became, the more wealth he had. As a homeowner, he was also able to borrow against the equity that was building without affecting the value of his house.

Once he started acquiring assets, he was well on his way to being wealthy. "Overall, housing equity makes up about two-thirds of all wealth for the typical (median) household." That meant that a house constituted 66% of the assets that made a person or family wealthy. Because only 41% of Blacks were homeowners, only 41% would have the foundation needed to build what made up almost 70% of wealth. In short, "the racial wealth gap is primarily a housing wealth gap." Due to his wealth building mentality, Papa's investment in real estate made him financially better situated than 59% of Blacks in America. Papa realized early on that building wealth was a choice, and that he could work for his money or make his money work for him.

As a man with a wealth building mentality, he said little, but his actions were loud. According to his sister, he often walked around thinking about what opportunities could make the family more money. He was just that industrious. He not only sought out opportunities, but he put those plans in action, often being a penny-pincher until he reached his goal. He was an avid and voracious reader, always taking in new information and he kept his eyes open for new ways to build wealth. He knew that wealth was possible for anyone willing to put in the work to achieve their goal and smart enough to set the right goals. He knew that homeownership would provide him a sturdy launchpad and allow him to use the money he would have used paying rent towards other assets.

Papa used the equity in his family's home to buy other assets, including rental properties, commercial property, college savings bonds, acres of undeveloped land in New Mexico and stocks. When Papa was ready to buy a bigger home, he was able to sell the home he built, for top dollar, to purchase another home with more space for his expanding family. Grandma and Papa decided to move from their home on the Eastside of Detroit to a home on the Westside of Detroit in 1989. Shortly after moving in to the new house, they decided to gift it to me, their first grandbaby.

Chapter 2: *Generational Wealth*

When my Papa decided to leave our new home to me in 1991, he was creating what is called **generational wealth**[6]. Typically, generational wealth is passed from parent to children, but can be passed from one family member to any other younger family member such as grandparent to grandchild, aunt to niece and so-on.

With all things being equal, wealth is passed down more in White families than in Black families and thus on average, Blacks have less generational wealth. "Among college-educated Black families, about 13 percent get an inheritance of more than $10,000 as opposed to about 41 percent of White college-educated families. The average amount is also drastically different: over $150,000 for White family inheritances, versus under $40,000 for Black families.[7]

In order to transfer generational wealth, one party typically leaves possessions to another party, the **heir**[8], to inherit after they die. Those possessions, or what they leave to the heir is an **inheritance**[9]. An inheritance is typically transferred from one party to another in one of two **testamentary**[10] documents: a **will**[11] or a **trust**[12].

A **will** is a legal document that a person creates in order to give instructions on how they want their valuable possessions to be distributed after they die. A will has to be evaluated by a judge to determine if it is legal and valid.

A **trust** is separate a legal entity that a person creates for the sole purpose of giving instructions on how they are distributing their valuable possessions when they die. The trust does not need to be evaluated by a judge, and if it is properly set up it can operate as an independent legal entity that acts on your behalf when you die.

If the person who passed away does not have a will or trust, then they are said to have died **intestate**[13] and the rules of inheritance are decided by the laws in the **jurisdiction**[14] where the person passed away.

To transfer assets via a will or a trust, it is typically acceptable to list and describe them in the testamentary document. For instance, "I Reese leave my three carat diamond necklace and stock certificates to Khloe." However, in order to **convey**, or transfer, any real estate, like a house or condo, one must completely execute a contract called a **deed**[15] which lists all the details of the transaction including the **grantor**[16], the **grantees**[17], the **consideration**[18], the legal description of the property, and the date when the transfer is completed. The contract must then be signed and dated by both parties and a witness. Most states also require that the deed be **notarized**[19].

If a person leaves real estate in a will, the probate judge who presides over the estate will issue the new deed to the grantee, after the probate proceeding. However, if the person leaves real estate in a trust, the grantor must deed the property to the trust. Once the property is deeded to the trust, and the grantor (also now the **trustor**) passes away, the **trustee** will have the power to create a new deed transferring the property to the **grantee** (also now the **beneficiary**). (*Note*: in property transfers, depending on what testamentary document you use, it is possible to fit into more than one legal description at a time; for instance, you can be a grantee of property, but if you received the conveyance via a trust, you are also simultaneously, a beneficiary).

Unlike most generational wealth transfers, my grandparents decided to convey their home to me while they were still alive. Although they had purchased the property in their own names in 1989, in 1991 Grandma and Papa conveyed ownership rights to me by creating a new deed. Grandma and Papa used a vehicle known as a **Quitclaim Deed** [20] to **convey** the house from themselves as the **grantors** to me, the **grantee**.

To make their decision known to the whole world, this quit claim deed was **recorded**[21] at the **Register of Deeds**[22] in the county where we lived, in Michigan.

Realizing that I was a **minor** at the time, and also considering the fact that they could both pass away before I reached the legal age to make decisions for myself, they transferred the property to me, **in care of** "c/o" their assistant pastor, Reverend Elliot, whose purpose was to serve as the **executor**[23] of transferring the property to me.

Leaving real estate for a child is actually a big deal, and my grandparents knew that their children were not the most responsible people. Rather than leaving one of my adult relatives as the executor, they wanted to appoint someone they thought would be trustworthy and accountable. They wanted to make sure that no one was able to steal the property away from me, so they chose an executor that they thought was honest, God-fearing and business-minded. (He wasn't the right choice, but we'll get to that in a later chapter.)

Although my grandparents conveyed the family home to me, I did not own it by myself. I could not have gotten upset about not being allowed to eat ice cream for breakfast, and changed the locks on them. Why not? In the 1991 deed my grandparents reserved a **life estate**[24] for themselves. A life estate is a legal way of dividing the rights of ownership of a piece of real estate between who owns it in the present, versus who owns it in the future. My grandparent's life estate gave them the right to own the home in the present, and would give me the right to own the home in the future, after they both passed away. Immediately upon the death of both my grandparents, my rights to the house would **vest**[25] in me and full ownership would be conveyed.

However, if only one grandparent passed away, the other grandparent would still have **tenancy**[26] for the rest of his/her natural life. The right to tenancy did allow the **grantor**, to sell or mortgage the property. However, they could only sell or mortgage the part of the rights that belonged to them. Since it was a life estate, my living grandparent could only sell the property up until the date of their death, whenever that might be. If the grantor, who only has a life estate, attempts to sell the present rights and the future rights to another party, the conveyance would not be valid because it attempts to sell rights in the property that no longer belong to them.

When I turned 11, Papa died and his life estate expired. My grandmother now had the only remaining life estate that was left in the house. She decided that she wanted to move from the house in Detroit to a new condo in the suburbs and sell the house to her daughter (my aunt).

There was just one problem, I still jointly owned the house with Grandma. Although it seemed logical just to ask me to sell the house, she couldn't. I was a child. Under the law, a contract signed by a minor is on its face **void**[27]. In order to protect the assets of children, Probate laws do not allow children who have received money, real estate or any other assets, to legally transfer or sell those assets without the court's supervision to legally oversee the transaction and to make sure that the best interest of the child is protected.

So, when my grandmother asked me, who was 11 years old at the time, to sign a quitclaim deed conveying our house to my aunt and took it to be recorded at the **Register of Deeds**, that deed was automatically **void**. I'm not sure who told her that the deed I signed as an 11 year old was not valid, but a month later, she hired a lawyer, Mr. Morad.

Teachable Moment: Oftentimes, people attempt to take shortcuts when dealing with their legal affairs, especially when the necessary process is time-consuming and can involve high financial costs. Shortcuts do not make someone a bad person; it just means that they don't know of a less-difficult way to accomplish their goal. When a person is low on cash, low on time, wanting to avoid the legal process or lacking concrete ideas on how to navigate the legal process, they generally will try to find an easier route. At the time, handling this matter outside of court seemed like an easier route to my Grandma. Eventually, she learned that she could not circumvent going to Probate court to address my ownership rights in the house which she wanted to sell.

Back in 1991 when my grandparents deeded the family house to me, they did not foresee a number of life-changing circumstances: my grandfather becoming very ill, my grandmother having to become his caretaker, him passing away at such a young age, their Detroit neighborhood becoming less desirable due to drugs and crime, a house being hard to maintain for an older widow, and the property dropping in value. Thus, they did not anticipate needing to ever move out of the home before both of their deaths. Since multiple events changed unexpectedly in my grandparents' lives, my grandmother wanted to be able to have the right to exercise full control over her property in the future. (*Note:* Another option that can be used so that grantors retain control over property is an **Enhanced Life Estate Deed** or **Transfer On Death (TOD)**, commonly known as a **lady bird deed**[28]. (However, this type of deed is not recognized in every state.))

When my grandmother hired Attorney Morad, he filed a **petition**[29] with the local **Probate Court**[30]. When a person wants to control the **estate**[31] of a minor or a handicap individual, they must file a **Petition for Appointment or Conservatorship**[32]. Once appointed, the **Conservator** can request that the judge enter a **Protective Order**[33] which would permit the Conservator to take a specific action regarding the property that belongs to the minor. A **Guardian ad litem**[34], is often appointed by the court to give a report on what they believe would be the best course of action to protect the minor's best interest.

A Guardian ad litem was appointed to review my estate. The Guardian ad litem evaluated the deed that my grandparents executed in 1991, and realized that my grandparents intended to gift me the legacy of homeownership. He suggested that my grandmother should place my name, along with hers, on the new condo that she purchased after moving from the house in Detroit. Probably, out of fear of having to go through the court process again, my grandmother asked for permission from the court to allow her to place the condo in a **trust** on my behalf, rather of putting my name on the deed as recommended by the Guardian ad litem. Although my grandmother did not complete the process to become my Conservator, the Probate Court Judge did enter a **Protective Order**. The Protective Order said that permission to sell the house would be granted to my grandmother, if certain conditions were met, including the establishment of a trust.

Once again, a **trust** is a legal document that a **trustor** creates so as to give instructions on how they want their valuable possessions distributed when they die. If the trust is set up properly, by the **trustor**, it can operate as a legal entity that acts on his or her behalf to transfer whatever he or she wishes to whomever they designate as a **beneficiary** and through whomever they appoint as the **trustee**. The trustee (or **successor trustee,** if the trustor also designates herself the trustee) should carry out the final wishes as if they were the living mouthpiece of the trustor. The laws that govern a trust vary from state to state, but as long as it is written according to the law of that jurisdiction, it generally does not need to be approved by a judge. However, the burden is on the trustor to choose a trustee who will manage their affairs E-X-A-C-T-L-Y the way they were instructed to. (Again, later.)

The trust that Attorney Morad drafted for my grandmother was **irrevocable**[35] (could not be changed) and it was funded. To **fund**[36] the trust, my grandmother's lawyer, created a quit claim deed that transferred the new condo from my grandmother to the trust. The deed was signed and notarized. All of these documents were executed. Thereby the trust would automatically transfer the rights to the condo to me upon my grandmother's death. I would merely then need her trustee to execute a new deed transferring the property from the trust, to me.

Although Attorney Morad in 1997 got permission from the probate court to start the process of selling the house, he failed to follow up with the court to request a hearing on whether the terms of the sale and the terms of the trust were acceptable. Mr. Morad dropped the ball on both. The court did not approve the sale nor was a final order signed by the judge. Mr. Morad did not record the deed transferring the condo to the trust with Register of Deeds. Instead, he put the trust and deed away and carried on with his merry life.

[*Note*: Unfortunately, sometimes, hiring an attorney doesn't mean that things are handled properly. If an attorney fails to meet the legal requirements of their job, they might be held liable for **malpractice**[37]. More on this later.]

Now, all of this may be quite complicated and hard to follow (and if it isn't, then you're smarter than most lawyers and some judges). I can say from experience that it is as complex as a law school exam from Hell. However, imagine trying to explain this story to an 11 year old! You probably can't! Neither could my grandma. She never said a word about all this to me, even as I sat next to her on her deathbed. She never explained to me that she and my grandfather had left me a house that she tried to sell to her daughter, and replace with her condo.

She never explained to me that her attorney, Mr. Morad, had all the important documents that I needed in order to receive the transfer of generational wealth when she passed away. She never informed me that she had taken out a reverse mortgage, and that in order to pay it off and redeem the condo, I would need to use the money from her insurance policies. This would have been what I call a **sunset conversation**[38]. A sunset conversation takes place when a person who strongly believes that they are at the sunset of their life, decides to share directions and information with an heir on how to carry out their wishes. A sunset conversation includes telling the heir where all the pertinent accounts are and where to obtain the necessary documentation from.

If you have elderly people who you are close to, I implore you to have a sunset conversation with them and ask them if they have a plan for creating generational wealth. Have them explain what that looks like and detail what their vision is for all the members of the family. Ask them who they want to carry out their wishes and where there documents are located for safe-keeping. Having a sunset conversation is very difficult because the human mind never wants to imagine losing someone that we love so dearly. Nor, are most people comfortable thinking about their own death, even though, for all of us, its guaranteed to happen. The only way to introduce a sunset conversation is to assure your loved one that you want their wishes carried out exactly as they say. It may even be helpful to record the sunset conversation on audio and video, in case there is ever a dispute about what was said or the state of the loved ones mental health. A sunset conversation can also act as a verbal **will** in court, if there is no written one.

Had my grandmother and I had a sunset conversation, I might have been prepared for what to do when she passed away. The one time that she attempted to initiate a sunset conversation via text, the year before she passed, I brushed off the idea.I didn't want to think about Granny dying. But Granny knew things about her health that I didn't.

Because we never had a sunset conversation, I was completely left in the dark, and had no idea what *her children* had in store for me. I was not properly given the opportunity to build generational wealth and carry on my grandparents' legacy because I started out completely uninformed on how to secure the transfer of wealth. I didn't know much about Attorney Morad, or whether he was alive. I didn't know that my grandmother had executed a trust and a deed that was in his possession. I didn't know that his deed was irrevocable.

I didn't know who to talk to, and I couldn't ask questions about things that I didn't know even existed. I was up the creek without a paddle!

Chapter 3: Education – The Key That Opens Doors

I recall sitting in a well-known attorney's office in Michigan crying because I had no idea of how to handle inheriting Granny's home. He looked at me and said, "Young lady, I honestly couldn't think of a better person for this to have happened to."

"What do you mean?" I asked through the tears pouring from my eyes. I could barely make out his face as I cried.

"Well, if you were a girl with no education, no skills, and no future, I would feel really sorry for you, but the fact is that you've very smart, very educated, and you will bounce back from this and it won't really hurt you."

I thanked him for his time, and I left his office.

"Was that supposed to be comforting?" I wondered aloud as I drove off, still wiping my tears. How could losing my inheritance not really hurt me?

Sure, I had gone to law school, but I had never stepped foot into a wills and trust class. I had also passed the Bar Exam, but the bar prep course hadn't really explore those topics in depth. And yes, I have run my own law firm, but I had never handled any estates cases. I barely knew what a trust was prior to my grandmother passing away in 2014, so all of my education didn't count for anything because this was not an area of law that I was familiar with. For all I knew, it could have been poly-turbo nuclear-dynamic molecular-fission biology (which I don't think is a real subject, but if it is, I know absolutely nothing about it either).

I had attended an excellent college, Michigan State University (**GO GREEN! GO WHITE!**), and I was pretty well-versed in how to navigate life with the skills that I learned while there. However, I wasn't clairvoyant, so I had no way of figuring out obscure facts from over 17 years ago. Nor did I know how to open an estate or have the court to enforce my grandmother's wishes. I was smart, thanks to Grandma and Papa, but I knew that I was in way over-my-head. Perhaps the attorney meant that being educated would equip me to build a life so that I wouldn't need Granny's house. After all, my grandparents had empowered me so that I'd always be able to take care of myself.

One of the ways in which they empowered me was by always stressing academic excellence. To my grandparents, higher education was a no-brainer. There was no question of whether I was going to college, only where. Like many Blacks who grew up working hard to escape poverty, my grandparents saw the value of higher education and taught me to always put school first. For my grandparents, college was not an attainable dream. They simply couldn't afford it. And for their children, it may have been a desire, but a college education wasn't all that common back then. In 1972, only about 26% of Black high school graduates attended college, compared to 32% of Whites.

When I came along, Grandma and Papa realized that the world was changing rapidly and they believed that education would be the key to unlocking great doors for me. Their views mirrored the views of many other parents during that time. According to the College Board in 2005, many people had a general sense that higher levels of education were associated with higher earnings and that college was a prerequisite for a comfortable middle-class lifestyle.

In 2001, closer to when I graduated from high school, 40% of all Black high school graduates and 45% of all White high school graduates attended college. With college attendance on the rise, it seemed that a college degree truly was the best option available to guarantee the best quality of life. My grandparents had pushed me to do my best academically, and had even purchased **college savings bonds** to help me with the cost of college. Based on the cost of college in 2003, those bonds might have actually been helpful. But that was 20 years ago, perhaps it is time to take another look.

How Much Does A Bachelor's Degree Actually Cost?

The price of going to college has been increasing since the 1980s. According to the National Center for Education Statistics, the average cost *per year* for the 2015-2016 academic year was just over $19,000 for a Bachelor's degree at a public university. The price jumps to nearly $40,000 for a private university. These costs include tuition, fees, room and board. Therefore, the average for all Bachelor's degree programs comes out to $26,120 per year. This brings the total cost of attendance to an astronomical total of $104,480 for four years. The comparable cost for the same Bachelor's degree in 1989 was ONLY $26,902 for all four years.[39] What people in the '80s paid for their entire degree, is actually what young people today will pay for one year of college. The price of college is literally skyrocketing.

When I graduated from high school, I wanted to attend Spelman College, a private women's college in Atlanta, and one of the most prestigious **Historically Black Colleges and Universities** (HBCU). Upon my acceptance, I was sent a letter with a Financial Aid breakdown for my first year.

	Cost of Attendance	Resources	Contribution
Tuition	$10,660.00	Parent Contribution	$5,008.00
Fees	$1,865.00	Spelman Need Based	$1,640.00
Room	$4,300.00	Federal Stafford Loan	$2,625.00
Board	$3,000.00	Federal Plus Loan	$21,245.00
Books	$1,610.00		
Personal	$2,046.00		
Transportation	$1,236.00		
New Student Fee	$170.00		
Loan Fee	$623.00		
Total Costs	$25,510.00		$30,518.00

While I was jumping up and down with excitement that I had been accepted to my first-choice college, my mother took one good look at the Award Letter and said, "You may need to go somewhere you can afford." My award letter expected my parents to contribute $5,008.00, which neither of my parents could afford. My award letter also expected my parents to sign for a $20,000 **Federal Plus Loan**[40] which would require someone to borrow the cost of my education on my behalf. Whether or not they would be approved for the Plus loan would be based upon their credit worthiness. Again, no one was able to help me, and I didn't want to place an economic strain upon my family. It was time for tough love and the hard truth: without scholarships, I could not afford to attend Spelman. My mother suggested that I consider my other acceptance letters and find a school that I could afford on my own.

Without taking money into consideration, I would have loved to have become a Spelman woman. However, Michigan State was a much more affordable option for me particularly because I was offered a number of in state merit-based scholarships.

In contrast to Spelman College, Michigan State University is a public **land grant university** (funded by the federal government). In 2003, the tuition for an in-state student was $6,412 per year.[41] Attending a public university as an in-state student versus a private university was nearly 50% less expensive. So, I decided that Michigan State was the way to go.

My first year costs:

2003-2004 Cost of Attendance	Michigan Resident Student
Tuition	$5,135.00
Fees	$821.50
Room & Board	$5896.75
Books & Supplies	$970.00
Personal	$1500.00
Total Budget	$14,323.25

If I had written this book 15 years ago, I would probably suggest that students be more open to attending a 4-year public university over a 4-year private college, but with the rising cost of tuition at a 4-year public school, even that would be poor advice to give out. At $14,460 for in-state residents, the total cost of attendance for my first year is still less than the price of tuition alone for a freshman attending MSU now. As my younger cousin is preparing to attend Michigan State University this fall, I was speechless when I realized that her annual costs are twice that of what I paid in 2003.

Cost of Attendance 2019 - 2020	Michigan Student	Out-of-State Student
Tuition	$14,460	$39,766
Fees & Taxes	$64	$64
Room & Board	$10,522	$10,522
Books & Supplies	$1,134	$1,134
Personal	$3,040	$3,826
Total Budget	$29,220	$55,312

How Does One Pay for College?

College prices are usually lower for a Bachelor's degree at a public university than a Bachelor's degree at a private university. The price is also lower for students earning a Bachelor's degree in their own state, than the price for **out-of-state students** (students from another state). But even the lowest price of an in-state, public institution, Bachelor's degree is too expensive if the student does not have a viable plan for paying for the cost of their education. Few people have the ability to work full- time to pay $20,000 or $30,000 per year for school in addition to other life expenses. At this point, if a student does not have substantial scholarships, grants, or reimbursements from a job, they may want to rethink their educational plan. I believe that borrowing upwards of six figures to pay for a Bachelor's degree is financially irresponsible. I would thoroughly advise students to buy themselves more time and consider attending a two year college, where they can take many of their core classes like (math, science, and English) and then transfer to a 4-year university. While attending the two year college, they should also be applying for scholarships.

Another option is to attend a two year college, to obtain an **Associate's degree** in a well-paying field with a high demand and then save up to pay for the cost of the four year degree. There are colleges known as community colleges or junior colleges, which offer a two-year degree called an Associate's degree. An Associate's degree is the first level of (non-vocational) post-secondary education that high school graduates can pursue. These programs offer faster and more affordable education. Although they can take a longer or shorter period of time to complete depending on the pace of study, they are generally half the workload of a Bachelor's degree. They are therefore, about half the price of a Bachelor's degree, and sometimes they are significantly cheaper, as well, because Associate's degrees are often provided by more affordable community colleges. Some urban and suburban school districts throughout the United States even offer dual enrollment programs, where high school students can take community college courses towards an Associate's degree before even completing high school.

Flexibility is also a popular motivation for earning an Associate's degree. Many on-campus and online Associate's degree programs are designed for non-traditional students: people with families, jobs, and busy schedules. The classes are taught in the evenings, weekends, or even online. Often, the courses of study prepare you for entry-level work in certain careers such as a physical therapist's assistant, occupational therapy assistant, ultrasound technician, dental hygienist, paralegal, air traffic controller, radiation therapist, nuclear technician, registered nurse, medical sonographer, and respiratory therapist. A number of these jobs start off making an average of $60,000 per year.

Scholarships

For those who have their hearts completely set on attending a four year university, it is critical that they seek out financial assistance. Scholarships are the best way to go! I am so grateful to my high school guidance counselors for pushing me to apply for scholarships and grants. They greatly assisted me in reducing my out-of-pocket cost for college. When I attended college, I had earned seven scholarships. These scholarships were dispersed directly to the school to cover my bill, and what was left over I got back in the form of a **refund check**.

Aid	Fall Award	Spring Award	Disbursed
David Elliot Schlr	$1500	$1500	3000
Ford Schlr	$1250		1250
Ford Schlr	$665	$665	$1330
Optimist Int'l Schlr	$500	$500	$1000
Mich Competitive Schlr	$650	$650	$1300
Mich Merit Award	$625	$625	$1250
Outstanding Student Schlr	$300		
Total Schlrs			$9430

There are millions of dollars in scholarships available to students every year and for every possible reason under the sun. I would certainly recommend that students seek out guidance counselors, college readiness experts, and financial aid advisors to help with finding resources to pay for college. Without them, the cost of college can be overly burdensome and almost impossible for the average student. If a student is still overwhelmed by the cost of college, I would advise them to seek out a scholarship coach. That smaller financial investment (usually under $1,000) can yield returns of tens of thousands of dollars in scholarships. Additionally, I would strongly recommend that students join scholarship groups on social media, look for scholarships associated with their extracurricular activities, and religious organizations. Students should also check to see if their parents' employers give scholarships.

Student Loans

During the spring semester of my first year, the amount that my scholarships did not cover came to nearly $3000. I supplemented my scholarships by taking out **student loans**[42]. After visiting the Financial Aid office, I learned that I could borrow $6,000 in **Stafford Unsubsidized loans**[43]. Although I was also offered $3500 in **Stafford Subsidized loans**[44], I turned them down and took the unsubsidized loans instead. Due to my lack of knowledge on how loan interest rates were calculated, I didn't realize that it was best to exhaust all of the subsidized loans that you are offered before accepting unsubsidized loans.

Loans	Fall Award	Spring Award	Disbursed
Stafford Unsub	$2625	$3253	$5878
Stafford Sub	$1750	$1750	0
Total Loans			$5878

Why? Loans that are **subsidized**[45] cost less. The **interest**[46] on the loan is subsidized by the government, so a **borrower** is only responsible for the amount of the loan that is the **principal**[47]. Therefore, if you have to borrow money to pay for college, it is best to borrow at the lowest cost possible. All Stafford loans are public loans which are offered and guaranteed by the U.S. Department of Education. They are typically cheaper than private loans that are offered by banks. Without proper financial education regarding the loans that I was offered, I made uninformed decisions that cost me thousands of dollars in interest.

Prior to taking out a student loan, a college freshman must undergo twenty minutes of online Entrance Counseling. This "counseling" is far more comprehensive now than it has been in the past, yet it is not comprehensive enough. On one page it says, based on your loan amount, your monthly repayment is expected to be $X, and based on this, you will need a job with a monthly salary of $Y. The unfortunate truth is that young people at 18, will likely overestimate what they will make upon graduation, underestimate how long it takes to find a job in their field, and underestimate how their monthly repayment will impact their ability to cover basic necessities. Concepts of financial literacy are typically lost on 18 year olds with no previous budgeting experience.

Due to me having taken AP classes in high school, taking three college classes at a local community college the summer after I graduated high school, and attending MSU year round, I graduated in just three years. Thus, I was able to shave off the cost of attendance for an entire year of college. Over the course of my three years at Michigan State University, I only borrowed a total of $18,095 in loans. Much of the student loan debt that I borrowed, I didn't really need, but I took them out due to my lack of financial literacy. Nonetheless, I consider myself fortunate. $20,000 pales in comparison to some of the debt burdens that I've seen young people carrying from their undergraduate years.

Graduate School
If my educational pursuits had stopped there, then my debt load would have been rather manageable. However, I decided that in order to become a Congresswoman, like Shirley Chisholm, I needed to head to law school. Although I didn't personally know any lawyers or have anyone who'd attended graduate school in my immediate family, I decided to

sit for the **Law School Admission Test** (LSAT). Law School was even more expensive because I was going straight from college. I did not have any money saved from working, nor did I have a company that would reimburse the cost of my education. For better or worse, I made the decision to borrow another $94,657 to attend law school.

Cost of Attendance		Resource	Contribution
Tuition	$30000	Federal Subsidized Loan	$8500
		Federal Unsubsidized Loan	$10,000
		Law Achievement Scholarship	$15,000
		Grad Plus Private Loan	$18,710

At the time, it seemed like a smart idea to me based on what I was told the average attorney made in their first year, but hindsight is 20/20. Even though I received a Law Achievement Scholarship that cut the price of tuition in half, I still had to come up with $30,000 for the rest of the tuition, books, housing, and living expenses every year. I started law school in the Fall of 2006 and graduated in the Fall of 2008.

Had I known that I would be graduating into the belly of the country's greatest economic catastrophe since the Great Depression, I would not have been so eager to sign up for almost $100,000 worth of student loan debt.

Yet, here I was, a law school graduate with no job prospects during the worst hiring freeze and mass layoffs that law firms had seen in decades. Most of my classmates were unable to find jobs, and those who were able to, were vastly underemployed. I can recall one of my classmates posting that she was so excited because she'd just been hired with a very well-known home goods company, and that she'd be using her law degree to help her in the grand task of folding towels! Not that there's anything wrong with folding towels (I personally believe there is an art to it), however, I don't think that Lisa wanted to invest $100,000 into legal her skills in order to become an expert towel-folder. If that had been the case, she could have gone to a trade school, vocational school, or an apprenticeship instead of blowing six-figures like it was Monopoly money.

Based on my hard-earned lesson, I believe that graduate school should be paid for with scholarships, corporate reimbursement plans, or from money earned while working. Taking on more than six figures of graduate school debt must be a calculated risk in today's economy. Prior to taking out graduate school debt, the job market should be analyzed thoroughly for your chosen field of study; you should be confident that the school has a substantial alumni network to help with locating lucrative job opportunities or you should already have a strong job prospect. You should also feel capable of repaying the loan within 7-10 years with income earned by the job you anticipate landing.

Trade School

But even this advice may not be financially sound in a matter of years. To be candid, as the cost of education seems to be doubling every ten years, trade schools, vocational schools and apprenticeships are actually looking like much more viable options than a traditional 4-year college degree or even graduate school, in some fields. The cost of attending college has become so exorbitant that only few can actually afford to attend without placing themselves into untenable amounts of debt. And with the shortage of trade workers, the demand for skilled labor is very high. Moreover, the educational costs are comparatively low, and the pay is high: so much so that, depending on the trade, it can be on par with graduate degree earnings. Furthermore, the work schedules are quite flexible, which creates a win-win situation for anyone that is willing to get their hands and (perhaps their knees) dirty.

At present, young men and women are attending trade school for little to nothing (depending on the trade), compared to the cost of a 4-year college degree, and being able to make $70-100K per year (before overtime). There are several unions to choose from including the Laborers', Electrical, Plumbers', Pipefitters', Operators', Glazers', Pole Climbers', Carpenters', and many others. As an apprentice, when you start off at roughly $20/hour, the contractor hiring you takes the rest of your pay and sends it to the union which puts it towards healthcare, education, 401K, and time off. After completing 8,000 hours or four years as an apprentice, your base salary practically doubles.

There are a number of other upsides to being a skilled trade worker. For starters, trade unions offer college credits (usually 50 credits) and the cost is free for union members. Joining a union is free, and dues are taken from your hourly wages. For an 18-year old, joining the union would allow them to be paid to learn skills instead of attending college where you pay to learn information and then look for work to build skills.

A number of women I know have found great success with other vocations such as cosmetology, which encompasses wig making, makeup artistry, eyelash extensions and eyebrow semi-permanent tattoos (micro-blading). These women have been able to earn as much as people with professional degrees, some charging up to $200 an hour for their work. If you aren't sure that college is for you, I would suggest earning a trade or at least a skill set. And if you ever decide to go back to college, you won't need to worry about taking out student loans because you'll be able to finance your own education.

Student Loan Debt Crisis

After all, the biggest issue with the cost of college is that the students who are borrowing tens of thousands of dollars really don't understand the value of the money they're signing away. When I took out student loans, it was as if I were paying for my classes with Monopoly money. Such large amounts just didn't seem real. When I clicked the "submit" button to pay my tuition I never fully understood the difficulty that could be involved with paying them back. By working to earn the money used to pay for one's education, a student will be more careful as to how and where they choose to spend and what value they will receive in return.

As the cost for higher education continues to rise, the number of graduates unemployed or underemployed is increasing drastically. Today, nearly two-thirds of all students depend on student loans, obtaining $27,000 in loan debt on average. Over 27% of borrowers are at least 30 days delinquent and nearly 10% are in serious default at any given time. Total student loan debt now represents over $1 trillion, which far exceeds total credit card debt.

These statistics paint a grim picture: that many young borrowers are in over their heads. Some borrowers even lack the means to repay the suffocating monthly repayments and simultaneously pay for basic necessities. A 2012 report found out that 53% of recent college graduates, or 1.5 million people under the age of 25 with bachelor's degrees, are either unemployed or underemployed. For those with jobs, the ability to repay can still be overwhelming. While the cost of a four year degree exploded to $104,480, real median wages only went from $54,042 to $59,039 between 1989 and 2016.[48] Thus the price of a degree has doubled but wages have not. The idea that student loan debt is a good investment is no longer an absolute truth.

If an entire generation of people are stymied in their ability to balance their student loan debt repayment and providing basic necessities so much so that they have little resources left to begin building their lives, the entire country will begin to feel the effects.

With over 40 percent of people age 20–29 years old carrying student loan debt, the present generation has become a nation of debtors. Based on current trends that number is set to only climb higher. The national delinquency rate is stark evidence that many Americans are struggling and will continue to struggle to repay their student loans.[49]

If you are having trouble paying your loans, you may need to rethink your repayment altogether. Check out options for forgiveness and see if you qualify. When paying off student loan debt, I have personally decided to pay off as little as possible over time using the Income Based Repayment plan, and ask that the rest be forgiven by the Public Service Loan

Forgiveness Program. When paying off student loans, its has not been helpful to attempt to wipe out my debt quickly. As long as the debt is in a repayment plan, even if the monthly repayment amount is set to zero, I am still eligible to be considered to have made sufficient payments for loan forgiveness.

The upside of using student loan debt relief, is that it frees up the rest of your available income to pay your bills. The downside of using debt relief is that the balance balloons with interest until it is paid off or forgiven completely. Before you consider debt relief programs, think about whether you have any reasons why it would be harmful for your debt to appear to be growing beyond a certain number.

Financial Literacy

Helping young Americans and their families learn how to make sound financial decisions about their education and how to pay for it is critical. Most young people are at the mercy of their socio-economic class when it comes to financial literacy. A parent can only teach children what they know, and oftentimes a poverty-mindset is passed down to first generation college students. If young people are provided with the tools of financial literacy and the borrowing agreements broken down into layman's terms and made digestible, a borrower should be able to comprehend calculations for cost broken down by semester, based on the expected date of graduation. Other factors, including a student's intended major and estimated entry level starting salary should be factored in college attendance decision making. Students should create a best and worst case scenario budget based on their expected earnings and repayment schedule. These calculation should explore what a student will need to make in their chosen career path in order to live comfortably while paying their loans, and it should include a forecast of the job market for their chosen field when they expect to graduate.

In reality, financial comprehension is a two-way street. You can lead a horse to the stream, but you can't force it to drink. When it comes to financial comprehension, you can lead a borrower to logic, but you can't make them think. However, providing this information will at least better equip a potential borrower with tools to make better decisions.

With proper education, some students may be forced to reconsider their majors, find in-state or less expensive schools, attend community or junior college, or survive solely on private scholarships, Pell grants and paychecks. But the end-realities of these sacrifices should end up best serving those same success-hungry young adults, otherwise being coerced into taking deep debt from institutions that routinely obfuscate the value of the degrees they offer. Many of these institutions are also guilty of providing little help to students hoping to find relevant work after they've matriculated.

A rise in borrowing and college cost escalation in the face of a compressing and more selective job market have resulted in no improvement for the financial security of most recent graduates. The entire system must be revamped. Otherwise, it will continue to damage our economy by indenturing talented students, who are our greatest renewable resource. This is not just an individual problem, but also a problem for the economy. With financial literacy taught to incoming freshmen, better decisions can be made that would likely result in a decline in the national student loan debt.

Chapter 4: *Saving For Wealth*

When the market took a turn for the worst and my law school classmates started posting on social media that they were taking jobs folding towels at home furnishing stores, I decided to make a risky move and hang my own shingle, rather than begging for a job that did not exist. In 2010, I started the Everson Law Office and began doing legal work for my friends in downtown Chicago. I represented my furrier who owned a top Fur Salon on Michigan Ave, a Playboy Playmate who was paid to make nightclub appearances, and pretty much everyone in between.

In addition, I worked on a local political campaign to continue exploring my interest in politics. While working on the campaign, I met an Illinois Congressman and shared my political aspirations with him. He wrote a letter recommending me for a Congressional Fellowship, and I was awarded the fellowship. If you read my first book, the B.A.B.E.'S Guide to Winning in the Workplace: You Don't Have to Compromise, you will know that the experience I faced was a very trying one, which involved sexual harassment, wrongful termination, and being blackballed (for all the intriguing details, grab a copy and fast forward to

Chapter 5). When my speaking up about sexual harassment resulted in economic assassination, I had to figure out how to survive while unemployed.

Emergency / Rainy Day Funds

Fortunately for me, my grandmother always told me to keep three months of expenses saved up in a **rainy day fund**[50]. To my credit, I had taken her advice and stashed double of that amount. I made it a point to live on a fraction of my meager fellowship stipend. I rented the least expensive apartment I could find (in a safe area). And when I found an even cheaper place ($500 less), I moved from that apartment to the cheaper one to save even more money! I was so excited about being able to save an additional $500 dollars a month, that I didn't care that it was half the size of my old apartment.

I loved saving money because I enjoyed seeing the number in my savings account grow larger and larger. It felt so good to see $10,000, then $20,000, then $30,000 in my bank account. I looked online to find a savings account that offered the most interest and incentives. I even opened a new bank account just because it offered a $250 bonus. I felt empowered knowing that I had available funds to build when the time came.

I also learned that Washington, DC has an Inclusionary Zoning **Affordable Housing Program**[51] that allows apartments to set the price of rent based on how much money you make, rather than the market rate. So, if the market rate is $2000, but you earned below $50,000 per year, (which many interns and fellows do) your rent could be as low as $1000. Locating similar programs in your area is critical to helping you save, particularly if you are just starting out in your career and taking a low-paying position to get your foot in the door. According to the book <u>The Millionaire Next Door</u> by Thomas J. Stanley, the amount you spend on housing should be no more than 30% of your income. Having read that book, I decided to find a place to live that I could cover with one and a half week's salary. Additionally, rather than taking the metro, I walked four blocks to work. I packed my lunch and avoided entertainment that required me to spend unnecessarily. In a city like DC, it was quite easy! There was too much one could do and explore for free, such as museums, botanical gardens, free outdoor concerts, and workout classes. I even signed up for a movie screening list and concert seat filler list that came with free tickets almost weekly. Reducing my fixed expenses and my discretionary spending allowed me to save nearly $1000 each month.

    The month after I got fired and was home surviving off of my emergency savings, my grandmother called me and said, "come home." Have you ever heard a mother's claim that they have eyes in the back of their heads? Well, my Granny could sense what was going on with me as if she had eyes following me at all times; I guess our hearts were truly connected. In January 2014, she called me to come home to Detroit, but I was too ashamed to tell her that I had been fired for reporting sexual harassment from my boss. I didn't want her to worry about me. I was convinced that I could find another job quickly. I knew things would work out with time. I hadn't exhausted all of the contacts I had made, and I was confident someone would hire me.

    Realizing that I was putting out money and bringing in none, I tightened up even more financially. I cut off everything I did not need to find work. Cable? Gone. Food delivery subscription? Cancelled. $100 hair appointments? Over and done. I cut my expenses down so that the only bills I had were rent (which was now lower based on my only income being unemployment insurance), cellphone, internet, renter's insurance, car note, and car insurance. I learned to do my hair and nails myself. After paying my bills each month, I had no money left, but I was safe to keep looking for work. To keep myself busy when I wasn't looking for work, I journaled about my experience with powerful men in the workplace. That journal went on to become an Amazon bestselling book, The B.A.B.E.'S Guide to Winning in the Workplace. But, back when I was unemployed and my checking account showed zero dollars after paying all bills and before buying food, I was on pins and needles wondering what to do.

    I was able to continue looking for work and writing my journal from January until May, when Granny called again and said, "Come home." Going home meant going back to Detroit, and to me that was a terrible idea — not because I had any particular issue with Detroit, (except for the blistering, long winters), I simply felt that returning home rather than finding the next opportunity would be an acceptance of defeat… an acceptance of failure… and an acceptance of the idea that the success I'd worked really hard to accomplish had been snatched from me. I was also left powerless to do anything about my perceived failure. I had felt this way for months as I pushed Granny's request out of my mind.

    But the last time in May 2014 when she told me to come home, it meant something different. Granny wasn't asking for me, instead she was asking for herself. Granny was asking me to come home to spend time with her, but I was so consumed with shame, and I couldn't see that before. That day, I felt a shift in my spirit and heard God say, "Pack up and go."

The voice didn't say move out, it just said "pack it up." So, I did something very bizarre. I packed up two suitcases with clothes, I took all the rest of my clothes and shoes out of the closets and packed them in boxes. I took all of the papers in my desk, all of my books and toiletries in my bathroom and packed them in boxes. I took all of the pictures on the wall down and packed them with the papers. When I was done, I packed all of the boxes in the front closet. Then I cleaned my apartment from top to bottom. It was spotless. My apartment was now fully furnished like corporate housing with a queen-size bed, a couch, TV and a dining set.

I kept going back and forth with myself on whether I should move back home, or just leave my things. My spirit said "Leave it." I loaded my suitcases in my car and headed for Detroit. A week later, a friend who had just had a baby called and asked if she could stay at my place. Because I had listened to the small still voice inside of me, everything worked itself out. I was able to send her the keys and be a blessing to her.

I had also just gotten a new job doing research for a lobbying firm and was informed that I could work remotely. When I arrived at Granny's place, I set up shop on a blow-up mattress in my old bedroom that still had hot pink walls from when I painted it in the 9th grade.

With my friend staying at my D.C. apartment, my rent was covered and I was able to focus on spending quality time with Granny. Granny was so happy to see me, and I was overjoyed to see her as well. It was always a joy to be in her presence. When I came through the front door, she said "Who loves you?" I replied, "You do!" and hugged her. She was a classy, stylish woman, even with the oxygen tank flanked behind her which helped her to breathe. She pulled it around daintily and effortlessly with hands that had a fresh set of French manicured acrylic nails. She was just as beautiful inside as she was outside, for a woman of seventy, she barely had a wrinkle.

We spent the next two months vegging out, watching our favorite shows on the Oprah Winfrey Network in our matching Victoria's Secret flannel pajamas. I tried to introduce her to a healthier diet than the fried foods and fast foods her daughters fed her. I cleaned all the junk food out of the house and purchased fresh fruit, vegetables, and healthy proteins. I took her to her doctor's appointments, dentist's appointments, to do her banking and to church. On Sunday mornings, she'd wake up at 6am, and I'd help her get dressed in order to be the first person to open the church. This was a routine that allowed her and the other church mothers to pray over the pastor, the members, and the church service that day. She loved her work as the Director of the Missionary Ministry. She was a praying woman and loved to serve God's people.

One day, Granny said she wasn't feeling well, and we went to the hospital. As usual, I'd sleep on the hospital bed with her. We called it our "spa getaway." We would go to the hospital, but instead of being sad or afraid, she'd go for two or three days, and when she was ready, we'd go back home. In the hospital, we had room service and people pampering her all day. Granny truly loved being pampered like the Queen that she was. The doctors and nurses didn't mind that I stayed with her the whole time. They were happy to see that she was well cared for. But during our last spa getaway, the doctors said that her lungs had completely shut down and there was nothing more they could do. I knew Granny was a fighter and she had often said that she'd outlive me, so I believed her. She didn't need lungs, she could live off sheer will if she wanted to. But unlike all the other times that I'd driven from DC and taken her to the hospital for our spa getaway, spent days watching TV, ordering room service and relaxing with our feet up, Granny wasn't going to make it back home this time.

Granny passed away on July 18, 2014. I was in disbelief, but I didn't even have time to grieve.

Death Can Bring Out the Worst in People
While she and Papa had amassed many valuable possessions from their multiple streams of income, including rental properties and businesses, when Papa passed away and Grandma advanced in age, her children decided not to carry on with the family businesses or take over the rental properties. As a result, those streams of **passive income**[52] dried up. Over time, Granny began to sell off some of her valuables in order to and care for her adult children who called on her frequently for financial assistance because they had not learned the wealth-building mentality that she and her husband practiced. Granny also gave many **charitable contributions**[53] to her church, which constantly needled its congregation for more money. As Granny's health began to fail her, her children continued to need her to bail them out, and her church bled her dry. She reached the bottom of her

savings and began liquidating her assets such as her timeshare, and she even took out a reverse mortgage on her condo.

The day Granny passed away, her pastor, now Bishop Elliot, came over for "the reading of the will." I sat in Granny's living room with her three adult children, as her pastor read out her last wishes. Bishop called the family meeting to order. He asked for Granny's will or trust. I handed the two documents from Granny's "funeral file" to Bishop and both were marked "Agreement of Trust." He asked, "Is this all?" I didn't know of any other trust documents.

My aunt, while looking down into her lap, said under her breath, "there is another one, but he..."

Everyone turned their head so fast to look to my aunt that they almost snapped their necks. Bishop cocked his head to the left and stared at her. Her siblings gave her a cold stare, and she went silent. I had no idea what was going on. Bishop began again, "If these two trusts are the only two here, then we will go with these."

One trust was dated 2007 while the other trust was dated 2008. Bishop said, "Since the 2008 version is the most recent, we will read from that one." He read the 2008 Trust which listed Granny's valuables and who she wanted to leave them to. Bishop said to me, "Granny has left you this condo, but my understanding is that it has a reverse mortgage that you will need to clear, otherwise it will go back to the bank."

My aunt erupted, "She may have left you the house, but I bought her this living room couch, so it's mine!"

My mother chimed in, "Well, I bought her this dining room table, so that's mine... And all of the artwork here is mine."

My aunt piped back up, "And those TVs are mine, even the TV stands, and I paid for that refrigerator."

At this point, my head began spinning. What in the hell was going on?

I was so disgusted by my family's greed that I was almost nauseous. Normally a calm and cool person, I was reaching my boiling point and things were quickly coming to a head. "What else do you want?" I demanded.

"Well, that air mattress that you're sleeping on is mine, and the white comforter you're sleeping on is mine too... And I need them because I have a guest in town." My aunt said snidely.

I didn't have the stomach for her pettiness. She was upset that she couldn't have what she truly wanted and needed; an inexpensive place for her and her children to stay, thus she began to lash out and grapple for whatever she could exert her control over. I could clearly see that she was resentful of my inheritance. I walked into my childhood bedroom, picked up the air mattress and threw it into the front hall.

But my aunt was just getting started with her pettiness, "I bought those dishes, I bought that juicer, those pots and pans are mine...." She said.

Bishop had kept silent during the exchange. When I sat down, Bishop continued reading.

Granny had also left me her heart-shaped diamond pendant. Granny left my aunt a timeshare in Mexico (that she'd already sold the year before), and her diamond wedding ring (which she had used as collateral for me to loan my aunt $2000 for the security deposit at her new place a few months prior). She left my mother a diamond tennis bracelet and a fur coat. She left my uncle her collection of silver coins. I expected Bishop to distribute the gifts and offer parting words; instead, I was told to unlock the door to Granny's room.

Then, things went haywire.

Instead of taking leadership as the elders of the family to assist and guide others through the grieving process, my aunt and uncle bolted past me, almost knocking me down and stormed into Granny's room. They opened the closet, grabbed the safe containing all of Granny's valuables, turned around and rushed out of the front door. Bishop sat there watching in silence while my aunt and uncle carried the safe out of the front door. I asked Bishop, "They're carrying the safe out of the front door, aren't you going to do something?" He did nothing to stop them, instead; he stood up to gaze out the window at the golf course across the street.

This could not be happening. Who were these people? They couldn't be my aunt and uncle? They must be some type of crazed zombies who had eaten my aunt and uncle's brain and took over their bodies, or were they? Perhaps, this was exactly who my aunt and uncle were, and I had just been oblivious to it for the last 27 years of my life.

Maybe I should have known better. If I had been able to talk things over with Granny privately, all of this craziness would have been anticipated. My grandmother's children had been a hot mess all of their lives. Granny's children were in their 50s and 60s, yet none of them owned property. None of them owned the homes they lived in or rental property. None of them had investments. None of them owned their vehicles. None of them had taken to heart the financial literacy taught by Papa to build with. Each one had been given at least two rental properties by their parents, yet none of them had used the properties to create other streams of income. Unlike my grandparents, who had a wealth-building mentality, their children had a **poverty mentality**[54].

Those with a poverty mindset will literally eat the seeds that were given to them for survival, rather than planting them — seeds that can grow and feed their entire family for years to come. My grandparents left an incredible blueprint for wealth, but their children ate their seeds (and were working to eat my seed too).

If I weren't careful, the blueprint for what would happen if I didn't save and be smart with money was staring me right in the face. When their mother died, death became a for-profit experience they needed to maximize to their benefit — this was because they had only learned how to work for money but had not learned how to make money work for them. Fortunately, I was on a different trajectory.

Chapter 5: Reverse Mortgages, Mortgages & Credit

I tried to stay focused on securing my inheritance. Bishop Elliot had said that Granny's house had a **reverse mortgage**[55], which I would need to clear. But what did that even mean? I didn't know exactly what a reverse mortgage was. Eventually, I learned… the hard way. On its face, it sounds like a special type of mortgage. Reverse mortgages have only been around since 1988, and since then they have wreaked a great deal of havoc in many communities. Many of our grandparents and parents got them without our knowledge and will unfortunately leave us to figure them out once they've passed away.

By definition, a reverse mortgage is a **loan**[56], and according to some, a **predatory loan**[57]. 95% of all Reverse mortgages are **Home Equity Conversion Mortgages (HECM)**[58] sponsored by the **United States Department of Housing and Urban Development (HUD)**[59]. When senior citizens (people over 62) own a home free and clear and have paid off their mortgage (or only have a small mortgage balance left), they are eligible to take out a HUD-backed reverse mortgage loan. The senior citizen can request to receive the money they've borrowed as a **lump sum payment**[60] spread out over a monthly basis, or on an occasional basis through a **line of credit**[61]. With this loan, the homeowner is borrowing against the **equity** in their home. The **collateral**[62] for the loan is the home itself.

The difference between a mortgage and a reverse mortgage is that the senior citizen <u>does not</u> have to make payments to repay the reverse mortgage. When the senior citizen passes away (or moves away from the home for more than a year) the loan is considered to be in **default**[63] and the loan is automatically due. The loan will also be considered defaulted on if the taxes or homeowner's insurance for the home go unpaid. The bank then has the legal right to take ownership of the home through a legal process known as **foreclosure**[64]. After the bank takes ownership of the house, the local sheriff carries out an **eviction**[65] to remove the senior citizen and/or their family from the home. The bank then sells the house to get the money they loaned back.

The reason that reverse mortgages are viewed as predatory is because the bank typically loans the senior a fraction of what the house is worth, and then piles on interest and fees which then balloons almost exponentially, so that by the time the senior citizen passes away, the amount owed is worth more than the house. If the family or heirs want to keep the home from being foreclosed on, then they are expected to purchase the home for the amount borrowed plus interest and fees, or at its **market value**[66].

When I inquired of Bishop Elliot and Granny's children how I was supposed to clear the reverse mortgage, I was instructed to take out a mortgage. But the thought of having to borrow to buy a house that was gifted to me didn't make much sense. Why would anyone want to take out a mortgage to buy a house in a city where they weren't planning to live. If I were going to go into debt, it should be for the house I chose to live in and not the house I was forced to save. Nonetheless, I started the process of calling the bank to see what steps I needed to take to avoid **foreclosure**.

The bank informed me that I would need proper authorization to talk to them on behalf of my grandmother's condo. In order to get the necessary authorization, the loan officer suggested that I go to court and open an **estate** for a person who had died **intestate**[67] (without a will or trust). Although my grandmother had two documents in her file cabinet that were marked "Agreement of Trust," neither of those trusts were accompanied by a **deed**, which meant that neither of those trusts were **funded.** And an unfunded trust could not govern or control the condo. (As I mentioned in Chapter 2, in order to transfer real estate into a trust, you have to transfer it with a **deed**.) Without a deed transferring the condo into the trust, I could not use the 2007 or 2008 trust to establish authority.

As directed, I went to the court and opened a **Decedent's Estate**[68]. Once I paid the filing fee, I had to decide whether to file an **application for an informal proceeding** or a **petition for a formal proceeding**. (Either choice allows a **personal representative**[69] to be appointed by the court.) When I opened the informal proceeding and obtained a personal representative, I reached out to Wells Fargo to inform them that I wanted to purchase Granny's home.

There was a small window of 45 days, which the bank made available to the family if they wanted to purchase the reverse-mortgaged home back. However, per HUD, the family is allowed to request three extensions. Right after Granny passed away, I left town to grieve and to escape her children and their madness. When I returned, I learned that I needed a court's authorization. So, I asked for the first extension. After the bank came to the condo and appraised it at $70,000, I asked for another extension to come up with the funds.

But there was one problem; I still did not have title to the condo. Although I had filed the paperwork to get authority to speak with Wells Fargo, I did not yet have ownership rights to her home. In order to obtain ownership rights through an unfunded trust that did not have a deed, I would have to request a hearing on her 2008 trust and ask the Probate Judge to give me **title**. Since the State of Michigan is an **heirs' state**[70], any property that Granny owned that wasn't governed by a will or trust would automatically be inherited by her heirs, in this case her children. If the asset left behind was real estate, the property could be sold and the profits will be divided by the number of heirs. That means that even if I spent my money to save Granny's house without having title to it first, a judge could later decide that the title belonged to Granny's children.

I didn't want to go through a lengthy court battle with Granny's three children over a question that had been well-settled during the reading of the will. I had already witnessed the extent they would go to because of greed. I did not need to refresh my memory. I knew they would still want title even if I paid off the mortgage. Realizing that I needed more time, I asked for a third extension.

After speaking with my attorney, he suggested that our family come together and sign a **family agreement**. He informed me that the family agreement was a legal document where the family gives up their right to ask the court for ownership or proceeds from the house. He suggested that the family agreement reflects the wishes that Granny wrote in her trust, that the condo would be left to me. He said it was the only way to avoid a dispute in probate court.

I drafted an agreement with the following email:

Dear Family,

As I move forward to take the steps needed to secure the Condo and salvage it from the reverse mortgage, I have asked that we come together and put in writing what was verbally agreed to in the presence of Bishop.

...

The family agreement that is attached below simply states the following: Granny did not leave a will, but she wanted me to receive the Condo, and as her children, you all agree that the property ought to be conveyed to me.

My goal is to do no harm to anyone else. I would like the same in return. Please sign and notarize the agreement and return to me or feel free to call, text or email any questions or concerns.

In Peace,

Reese

When I presented the family agreement to my aunt, she refused to sign it. When I presented the family agreement to my uncle, he refused to sign it as well. But even more, when I left my aunt's house after dropping off the paperwork, I heard my uncle say to my aunt over the speakerphone, "Don't worry sis, we'll just buy the condo when it goes to foreclosure." I was speechless! My family members had no intention of seeing me inherit my grandmother's house. Instead, they were waiting on it to go foreclosure so that they could buy it.

I reached out to Pastor to see if he'd help get my aunt and uncle to sign the family agreement. Later I got a call that Wells Fargo was coming to do an appraisal. In May of 2015, Wells Fargo sent out an **appraiser** to assess the value of the condo. The appraiser determined that the condo was valued at $70,000. I decided to come up with the $70,000, but I knew I had to act quickly.

When I called the bank to request an extension so that I could come up with the money, Wells Fargo informed me that my aunt had called the bank and agreed to turn over the condo to the bank **deed in lieu of foreclosure**[71] and that they were refusing to grant the third extension. When you turn over the condo, you allow the bank to have ownership of the house without having to go through the foreclosure process, basically evicting yourself from the home. Since we had not yet gone through probate to have a judge grant me title, I did not have control. But neither did she. She was making decisions regarding the condo as the successor trustee of Granny's 2008 trust, even though the condo wasn't deeded to the trust and it did not have authority over the condo.

Despite my aunt running interference, I kept working to purchase the condo. Thanks to years of financial literacy self-help books, I had great credit and was currently taking a first time home-buyers course that helped first time homebuyers with their closing costs. The first time home-buyer's class had pre-approved me and I was working to apply for a **mortgage**[72]. What's a mortgage?

A mortgage is a loan given to a bank by a person, in order to borrow the **purchase price** of a home. The person giving the mortgage to the bank uses the house as **collateral** on their promise to repay. Mortgages are not a right, and they are not available to everyone. Banks have the right to decide who is eligible for a mortgage based on who they believe will repay their loan. Banks are supposed to base a borrower's ability to repay a mortgage on their **credit history**, their **debt to credit ratio,** the amount of debt they currently have, their other assets, and their income. In order to give a mortgage on a property, the buyer of the property must sign an agreement promising to pay the bank back the amount they borrowed to purchase the property.

When I found out that my aunt was turning over the house to the bank, I was devastated. I was so close to saving the house from foreclosure. My credit was excellent and my new employer was prepared to help if needed.

If you read The B.A.B.E.'S Guide to Winning in the Workplace, you know that I'm a huge fan of Suze Orman. I first learned of Suze Orman when I was a 16 year old high school senior. I read her book For the Young, Broke, and Fabulous from cover to cover. I read the chapter she wrote on having good credit and took baby steps every week until I put all of her recommendations into place. By the age of 17, I was able to buy my first car with no **cosigner** because I had excellent credit. It's a great book worth thumbing through, but I'll give you my own top ten tips on how I've kept an excellent credit score (over 700) for the last 16 years.

Reese's Top Tips for Fabulous Credit

1) Read Your Mail

This tip seems easy and simple but most of the debt that we have or dings to our credit come as a result of something that came to us in the mail that we did not open and read, whether it was a medical bill, shutoff notice from the cable company, or a student loan collection letter. Once I open my mail, I organize all bills by company and due date.

2) Make a List, and Check it Twice

At the first of each month, write down all the bills that are due AND their respective due dates. Being late once will ding your credit something terrible, and those dings add up.

3) Check Up On It

At least once a year, pull your credit reports for free from Equifax, Experian, and Transunion and see what's on there.

4) Stay Informed

Sign up for a free credit monitoring service offered by one of the credit bureaus, your bank or a third party financial app like Mint.

5) Pick up the Phone

Okay, so you missed the payment window or you know you're going to be late, pick up the phone and ask the company to extend the grace period and remove the late fee. You'd be surprised what picking up the phone to ask for a bit of breathing room will do.

6) Dispute, Dispute, Dispute

When you pull your credit report, make sure that everything there is supposed to be, and if it isn't dispute dispute dispute.

7) Every "No" is a Starting Off Point for Negotiation

Reese's Top Tips for Fabulous Credit

If you have an outstanding debt that you think should be lowered, call the creditor and ask if they will waive some of the fees or penalties. Removing extra unnecessary cost will help you pay the debt off faster.

8) Let's Make a Deal

As a former bill collector (my first job in high school), I learned that bill collectors buy your debt for pennies on the dollar and hope that you'll pay it off in full. Therefore, if you have a collection due, they will likely accept less than what you owe. When dealing with a bill collector, it's about settling the debt, and not paying it in full.

9) Don't Negotiate with Terrorist, or Bill Collectors

Using good money to settle bad debt is a bad idea. If you can help it, never address debt with debt collectors. Go back to the source. If you have medical debt, go back to that actual office and pay them. If you have an outstanding balance with the cable company, go to them and pay it. When you pay something off through the collections agency, it is reported to the credit bureaus as "Collections - Paid Off" which is still a negative ding to your credit report and will lower your FICO score.

10) Lay it Away on Pinterest

More often than not when we spend money its on impulse buys. Companies have gotten very good about figuring out the science of what makes you spend and they know how to position things so that you feel you can't live without it. But the truth is, you can. In order to be less of an impulse shopper and more of a saver, it is best to spend money strategically. If you know that you have $400 in discretionary money each month, you can't blow $500 on a pair of shoes. However, if you see the shoes and they're calling your name take a picture of them. Get the make and style of the shoe. Try them on, make sure they fit, note what size you wear in them, then go on Pinterest and add them to your "Things I want to Buy" page. When you get home, look for them online for less than $500. Price compare and wait for a deal!

Let's be honest, most of us would like to believe that we have some level of discipline when it comes to spending. But the truth is that we all give in to the pressures of **conspicuous consumption**[73] more than we realize. Everywhere we go, we are being sold something. There are billboards on buildings, sale signs placed in the windows as you walk by shops, and even ads inside the subway and bus stop shelters. Even if you didn't leave your home, the advertisements still find their way to you via tv commercials and radio jingles — selling you all sorts of things that you probably don't need.

And the advertisements aren't just for products like shoes, lipstick, and earrings. No, it is far deeper than that. When products are marketed to us, its no longer about a product that you have to buy, it is what the product can transform you into. The right pair of shoes will transform you so that you are "cool and chic" like Rihanna, the right lipstick can make you "sexy and irresistible" like Beyonce, and the right earrings can make you "classy and rich" like Ciara. The items we are sold these days attach themselves to our self-esteem and self-worth, which can make it much more difficult to say "no", even when you know you don't need it.

The other issue with building financial discipline is that our generation has become overly comfortable with borrowing. Unlike those raised before 1950, we buy everything on credit. The issue with spending money and buying things on credit cards is that it makes everyone feel like they can afford more than they actually can. My Papa didn't believe in using credit to buy anything other than property, because it gave him a false sense of wealth. When Papa spent money, he paid cash so that he always knew if he could afford something or not. Taking the cash approach can be cumbersome and dangerous, so rather than walking around with a purse full of hundred dollar bills, I suggest leaving the credit cards at home and only carrying one card with the discretionary amount you that are allowed to spend on it. That's right, give yourself an allowance, and stick to it!

The more you take the delayed gratification approach, the more disciplined you'll become with money. When you cut down your spending, you'll be able to increase your savings. After all, to build wealth "it's not what you make, it's what you keep." Financial discipline is the one secret ingredient of generational wealth. When you are disciplined with $500, you can learn to be disciplined with $50,000 and even $50 Million.

Being Able to Buy It Doesn't Mean You Can Afford It

When I worked for Congress, I decided to use my excellent credit to take advantage of Nissan's no-money-down promotion. I needed a car to get back and forth to church with. I didn't care for the Metro and was tired of taking $20 Uber rides each way to church on Sundays and Wednesdays.

At $80 a week and $320 a month, I was better off paying $199 so that I could come and go as I pleased.

At the Nissan dealership, the salespeople were giving me the runaround, so I took that opportunity to go to lunch. While I walked around the neighborhood, I strolled past the Mercedes dealership and decided to drop in and take a picture of my dream car. I wanted a new picture for my vision board.

When I got inside, I walked up to the car of my dreams, opened the door and hopped inside. I turned my head to see a salesperson approaching. I asked him to take my photo.

The salesperson said, "This car was made for you!"

I agreed. The buff white exterior contrasted with my chocolate skin perfectly.

He asked, "Are you in the market for a car?"

"Yes sir, I am" I said.

"Which one are you interested in?"

" A Nissan Altima," I answered. Nissan was currently running a special for $199 a month with no money down. Being the budget-ista that I was, that price was just what I had in mind.

He looked at me and laughed. Then, he hit me with the best sales line I have ever heard in all my life:

"You don't look like a Nissan girl to me…. You look like a Mercedes girl."

Well, of course, that made me feel all kinds of fabulous. I liked the idea of being associated with high-quality German engineering.

But I responded with my truth. "I am, but I have a Nissan budget."

Because of my ability to delay gratification, I was willing to settle for a picture in a Mercedes that I could upload to Pinterest or paste to my vision board. Even though I knew that if I spent from my savings I could afford a Mercedes, I didn't have to own one unless I could drive it for the same price that I would pay for a Nissan.

As I got ready to leave, the salesman said, "Let me see what I can do."

The salesman and I spent the next few hours going back and forth about how much I could afford to spend and how much I could afford to put down as a down payment, but I held my ground. I could pay $199 a month with no money down. Period. After all, I was living on a very meager stipend at the time. After he tried to squeeze me for a dollar here and there, he finally accepted that I wasn't going to budge.

Due to my excellent credit, the salesman said that I was approved, but since I couldn't increase my budget, we remained stuck in negotiation. The salesman was convinced that I could find a thousand dollars to put down from somewhere, while I was convinced I wasn't going to spend a dime more for the Mercedes than I would have for the Nissan. He got up and walked me from the new car section to the used car section. I wasn't fazed by the idea of driving a used Mercedes. I knew that cars **depreciated**[74] approximately 40% once they were driven off the lot, so if I got a car that had been used for one year, it would still be a "new" car at a lower price. To even my own surprise, I drove off the lot around 8 PM in my shiny new Mercedes feeling satisfied that I'd been able to score a luxury vehicle on a Nissan budget.

Typically, financial gurus will tell you that a **car lease** is a terrible idea. They'll say that it's the same as throwing money down the drain, which has much truth. An **auto lease**[75] also allows people to drive more car than they can afford to buy. It's the equivalent of renting, but with a car. Rather than buying a brand new compact car like a Ford Fiesta, Chevrolet Spark or a Nissan Versa for approximately $15,000, and riding it until the wheels fall off, most of us would prefer to lease a Mercedes for $18,000. Generally, people would rather get the nicest car that they can rent, rather than the cheapest car that they can buy. To open the list of potential customers up to those who have Mercedes taste and a Nissan budget, car dealerships and financing companies got together to create auto leasing. Leasing is priced so that it costs the same to lease a nicer car as it costs to buy a more economical compact car. Like with renting, you have no equity because you don't own the car and can't sell it. On the other hand, there is something to be said for a young, single lady with no automotive intelligence and no uncles who work as mechanics having a reliable car that is still covered by warranty. Leasing also has tax write-off benefits if you own a business.

I believe that if you can get the cost of the lease down to a lower amount, it may be worthwhile if you aren't able to afford the **cost of ownership** and need a car that's still relatively new and covered by warranty. While ownership is always preferable, people usually don't explain that ownership comes with a higher price tag because of the maintenance and upkeep involved in it. When you own your car and the warranty expires, you have to either buy a new warranty or pay for each instance where something on the car needs to be fixed or replaced. Replacing a motor or a transmission is part of being a car owner. Also, taking the car to the mechanic repeatedly for a $200 diagnostic test is also part of ownership. If you're not good under the hood or related to a mechanic, owning a car can be full of unexplained drama.

But keep in mind, leasing higher end cars is often more expensive than the sticker price or the price advertised because maintenance is rarely factored in. When you lease a luxury car, it requires luxury upkeep (which is often upwards of $200). The Mercedes oil change known as the "A Service", costs about $200, and the "B Service," on average, costs $600. When you have a luxury car, your tires can cost over 4 times as much as regular tires. It is the same with other luxury goods.

If you decide to buy a Rolex because you're feeling fancy, that's fine. But every few years, a Rolex watch has to be maintained and cleaned on the inside which often costs over $600. And don't make the mistake of leaving the dial open while washing your hands, or you might be on the hook for $4000 worth of water damage, just like I was. What happens when you can't afford to maintain expensive luxury items? They become a waste of money and you likely have to sell them or turn them in at a cost.

However, if you are able to afford high-end luxury items and their maintenance, then that's a good thing, because they typically hold value much better than lower priced items. A Rolex watch, a Mercedes Benz car and a Chanel purse all tend to hold value compared to their basic counterparts, if they are well maintained. But be careful: not all luxury items fit into this category. And when spending your money, you have to do the work to know how well items hold their **resale value** or how quickly the item typically depreciates. You also need to research as to whether the amount you're asked to spend is a steal or a bad deal.

What time is it? It's time to check your savings account to see if you're building your assets or racking up liabilities. I repeat: Just because you can afford to buy it does not mean you can afford to maintain it. We shouldn't spend money just because things make us feel good. The day you disconnect the wires that connect the way you spend money to your feelings of emotional validation, is the day you're ready to start building generational wealth.

Chapter 6: *Real Estate*

Speaking of emotional shopping, I had to decide what to do about Granny's condo. Based on my years of financial discipline and experience with negotiating deals, I knew that it would not be a bad idea to purchase Granny's condo as long as the price was right.

I broke out my cell phone, opened up an app called **Karl's Mortgage Calculator,** and began punching in the numbers. Just because I could afford to buy a condo in the suburbs of Detroit didn't mean that it was a worthwhile purchase. At first blush, I was willing to spend over and above $70,000 to keep Granny's condo since I was emotionally attached to it.

Attached to a condo? How? Well, I'd lived there with her since I was 11 years old. Being inside the condo felt like being wrapped inside a baby's blanket. I felt that Granny's spirit was somehow lingering in the house and when I was there; truly, it gave me a feeling of peace. All the amazing memories I shared, and the times we spent laughing and singing would float to the surface as I spent the day thinking about her. All of the unconditional love she gave me would ooze from the walls. You can't put a price tag on that!

Or, can you? If I let all of those beautiful memories influence my decision, then I would be making an emotional purchase. The real question was not whether I could afford to buy the condo, but whether I could afford to maintain the condo. While the cost of maintaining a home is mostly fixed, the cost of maintaining a condo can change without notice due to the condo having a **Homeowner's Association fee**[76] that is set by the condo's Board of Directors. Condos also have the ability to charge special assessment fees to cover any number of expenses that they want the residents to shoulder. Having lived in apartments in three different states in the last six years (an apartment in college, an apartment during law school, and an apartment during my Congressional Fellowship), I had yet to buy a home and didn't know if purchasing a condo with undefined expenses was a good investment idea.

Then a friend from Los Angeles called. I shared my dilemma with him and he suggested I give AirBnB a try. At that time, I had never heard of AirBnB, but I decided to give it a try. I went on the website, took a few pictures of Granny's place and posted them.

As soon as I posted the condo, I got two hits for a reservation. I accepted the reservations, cleaned up, left my keys with a friend who agreed to clean after each guest, and I headed back to DC.

I didn't know it then, but I had just created my first piece of rental income with a property that I didn't even own yet. Within weeks, I had three reservation for guests who would come and stay for 3 weeks and pay $2000 each.

Buying the condo made sense if I listed it as a furnished executive rental apartment or rented it to semi-long term guests on **AirBnB**. I would be able to make at least $2000 per month and cover the cost of the mortgage, the Homeowners Association (HOA) fees, **property taxes**, and the utilities. After a few years of aggressively paying off the mortgage, I would have the property free and clear as an asset for as long as I owned it. If I choose not to pay off the mortgage quickly, I would pay more in interest, but it would still be a lucrative deal.

Buying a $70,000 condo using a traditional 30 year fixed rate mortgage with a $2000 down payment at a 5% interest rate would give me a mortgage payment of $365.00 per month. The monthly HOA of $572.00 plus the $3000 annual property tax would amount to a monthly expense of $822 for a grand total of $1187.04. Presuming that I was able to keep the utilities and cost of supplies under $350 per month, my final total would be $1537.04. If I made $2000 from renting the place, I should have been able to pocket approximately $462.96 each month.

By purchasing the condo and converting it to a rental unit, I would be creating a stream of income that would allow me to eventually save more money. Based on my calculations, buying the condo was a good deal for $70,000. The condo was located in a suburb of Detroit, which was being gentrified, and its property value was expected to increase. That meant my equity would also increase as well. Not only would I have the value of the property, but I'd also have monthly rental income, a win-win.

This is the magic of generational wealth and the value of receiving real estate as an inheritance. It can suddenly and completely change your financial reality and provide you with a nest egg, and if positioned properly, a sustainable stream of income. Inheriting Granny's home would put me in position to have rental income and pull down the equity in the condo to buy more property in metro Detroit. With her home as a stepping stone, I would be able to build a mini-empire of real estate, just as she and Papa had.

With the **cost of living**[77] rising drastically, many young people feel that they are priced out of homeownership, particularly in big and middle-sized cities. Combine the rising cost of living with the effects of the Great Recession, and it's easy to see why millennials' wealth levels are 34% below where they most likely would have been if the financial crisis of 2008 had not occurred. Add the rising cost of rent or buying a home to the rising cost of college and childcare, and you'll find that many millennials feel they aren't able to keep up with the cost of living, let alone save money. In 2019, over half of millennials reportedly relied on money from their parents to get by. Those born in the 1980s are currently at the greatest risk of becoming the "lost generation for wealth accumulation."[78] In order to find more reasonably priced places to live, young people have relocated to cities that are less populated with lower costs of living like Detroit, Baltimore, and Baton Rouge in order to play catch up.

Investing in Real Estate

Twenty years ago when my grandparents were investing in real estate, they went down to City Hall and purchased residential and commercial properties from the tax foreclosure sales. Today, that opportunity is still available. Tax sales are often a great way to get started with investment properties for a really low price. One key downside is that you have to do a great deal of research on the quality of the property and into the title to be sure that the property isn't encumbered by any other debts, liens or owners. If you buy a property with **cloudy** title it can come back to bite you. (More on this later.)

Let's Pick Up Some Rent

When I was a little girl, my Granny would take me with her and we'd run her errands together. Because she was a businesswoman and a landlady, most of our errands involved conducting business of some sort. Specifically, I vividly recall the day I was in the backseat of her Crown Victoria and asked her if we could go to Toys'R'Us because I wanted a new toy. Granny, undoubtedly aware that I had enough toys, informed me that she didn't have any money on her. To which I replied, "Well, let's go pick up some rent!"

Even as a little girl, I connected being able to have disposable income with a stream of income. Each time we collected rent from one of Granny's tenants, I was afforded a trip to Toys'R'Us. If I were able to purchase Granny's condo for the right price, it would certainly become an asset that I'd be able to use to take my own children shopping for toys. I reached out to the bank to let them know I was ready to move forward with the process.

The process of purchasing rental property can be tedious because you have to search for a property that is a solid investment. It has to be priced low enough for you to be able to make any necessary repairs or upgrades and still make a profit from either renting the property or selling it (which is called **flipping** property).

Since I had already identified the property, my work was cut down drastically. However, searching for a property in your budget is only the beginning because once you pick out a property, you have to determine what it is actually worth by having an **appraisal** done. Once the appraisal is done, you have to get an **inspection** to check the property for issues. The property must be inspected for any structural issues, water damage, mold, leaks in the roof, flooding basement, cracks in the foundation, and so on. Further, you must run a **title search**[79] on the property to see if there are any tax liens, construction liens, water bill liens, etc.

The home inspection is a visual examination of the physical structure and mechanical systems of the house. Unlike an appraisal, which determines the property's value, an inspection will determine the property's condition. Home inspections help you to make informed decisions by determining if there are any major defects that would cause an unexpected financial burden. The home inspection report will usually cover the foundation and basement, crawl space, roof and gutters, exterior finishes, electrical and heating, ventilation and air conditioning, plumbing, floors, walls, ceilings, attics, kitchen, bedrooms, and bathrooms.

If you successfully get through all of these checkpoints, your realtor can make an offer on your behalf or you can buy from the owner directly. Typically, there is a back-and-forth negotiation on the sale price of the property or the fees for the sale of the property and deciding who will pay for repairs, closing costs, and any owed taxes. Once the fees and cost are agreed to, the buyer has to come up with the funding via financing or cash purchase. To apply for financing, i.e. a mortgage, the lender will usually need to verify employment, verify assets, appraise the property and perform a title search. In some cases, it's a good idea to take out title insurance.

The buyer then puts down a deposit called an **earnest money deposit**[80] which is typically 1-5% of the sale price. If the buyer can't come up with the funding within the agreed time, they can ask for an extension. If they don't, they risk forfeiting their earnest money deposit.

Once the buyer is ready to proceed, the buyer and the seller will schedule a time to come to the table and complete the sales transaction in a process called a **closing**[81]. Prior to the closing, the buyer should receive a **Truth in Lending Statement** (TIL)[82], and a **Good Faith Estimate of Closing Costs** (GFE)[83].

When you arrive at a closing, you will meet with the settlement agent, receive a settlement statement, Truth in Lending Statement, the note, the mortgage, survey, pest inspection, appraisal and flood certification, the deed of sale, affidavits and disclosures, the title package, and any other necessary documents.

Investment Properties

In this day and age, buying one property at a time to fix and rent it may not provide the **return on investment**[84] (ROI) that you're looking for due to the rising cost of real estate and the amount of time it takes to actually make a profit.

If you're in the market for your first investment property, and get a good deal on a single family home with an owner-occupied mortgage and close on the house, the amount of passive income that you can make is still pretty low. And with an owner-occupied mortgage, you have to live in the property for some time before you can use it as a rental unit. Also, the amount of work that you'll have to do to upkeep one unit often outweighs the profit that you'd bring in. Another option that could provide more value would be a **multi-family building**, or multi-unit, which could be a duplex, triplex, or quad. When working to build generational wealth, property with more than one dwelling can save you time and money, thereby allowing you to fix one unit while occupying the other.

If you're currently renting and looking to become a homeowner, why not settle on a property that will provide you with a return on investment from the very start? A single family home provides no income until you decide to rent it out or put it on the market. However, a multi-unit can make you money as soon as you purchase it if it already has tenants or if it is **turn-key**[85]. So, in addition to building equity for the home you own and live in, you will also be able to create streams of income through rental income.

Although the purchase price of a multi-unit is much more expensive than the price of a single family home, if you're willing to move into one of the units, you can qualify for an **FHA loan**[86], which only requires a 3.5 % **down payment**[87].

The key to having a wealth-building mindset as opposed to a poverty mindset is to see every opportunity as an investment of either your time, talent, or treasure. Instead of looking for a home, those with a wealth-building mindset look for a property. When you begin to view purchasing land as property, the deciding factor becomes **the multiple gross of rent**[88] minus the amount of work needed to make the property rentable, instead of some arbitrary number set by a seller based upon what they feel the property is worth.

If you're overwhelmed, there are tools and resources out there to help you along the way. There are two ways that most people get help: 1) a real estate coach or class like Than Merrill's Fortune Builder, Phil Pustejovsky's How to Be a Real Estate Investor, or Daymond John's Success Formula. Typically, these classes offer you a chance to attend a free seminar to learn how to invest in real estate with "no money down." The seminar is basically multi-level marketing. The free seminar speaks from a 1000 foot view of real estate investing. All of it sounds good, but almost none of it is actionable. If you want to learn more, you can pay anywhere between $200-2000 to attend another seminar. The next seminar offers an 800 foot view, and almost none of the information is actionable without additional tools or contacts. Then, if you're still eager to learn more, you can attend another seminar for $350-3500 for yet another session of semi-accessible information. All the invitations usually lead to a buildup for the actual product which you can purchase access to for $500-15,000, which also promises to teach you how to locate good investment properties and how to get approved by a lender. How you actually apply the information you've learned is now totally up to you. Whether you succeed or fail, they are not overly concerned because you've paid your money and there are no refunds.

Another option includes working with a turn-key rental property company, such as High Return Real Estate, which will provide you with a number of properties that have already been fully rehabbed and are already **cash flow positive**[89] (net profit minus the mortgage). The companies will provide you with a listing of homes that have been "acquired, rehabbed, inspected, and tenanted," and all you have to do is choose the one that fits your budget. Although the property has a mortgage and a net profit, the properties may have already been bled dry of any available equity by the investor as they've typically been **refinanced**[90]. Also, these properties often come with a six month to one year warranty, and after a year, you're responsible for replacing anything that goes wrong. Generally, you can be on the hook for replacing a major system in the home, which may be hard to do once you've maxed your budget to be able to afford a turn-key property in the first place.

A third option, one that I have personally decided to explore is working with a hands-on Real Estate Portfolio Trainer. Like a personal fitness trainer that helps build your muscle, a real estate portfolio trainer helps real estate investors build their portfolios from the ground up. A real estate portfolio trainer will typically help you locate a property, walk you through the process of obtaining financing for the property, provide a team that will rehab the property, acquire all the materials and supplies at cost, and then hold your hand from purchase to tenants —— for a fee. The fee can be set by the trainer, and is usually a percentage of the rehab. With this option, you will not only have residual income from the rental, you will also retain full equity of the property after repair.

Chapter 7: *Insurance is Your Friend*

With Wells Fargo refusing to grant me the third extension, that I needed to complete the **short sale**[91], my Granny's home was in immediate danger of being foreclosed on. At that point, I didn't know what to do. I had tried to follow the attorney's advice to settle things amicably with the family agreement, but my aunt and uncle seemed dead-set against me inheriting Granny's condo. They had even started sending someone over to pack up her things in preparation for the foreclosure.

That night, I went to bed crying in complete despair and exhaustion. I desperately needed to talk to Granny. She was the only person whom I knew who had dealt with multiple real estate transactions. I needed her guidance on how to get the short sale done, how to finance it, and how to decide how much to put down. Although Granny had a wealth of knowledge she and I had never discussed real estate. Most of all, I was crying because I didn't know how to obtain title over the property and didn't want to battle with her children in Probate court. I climbed into her bed and fell asleep. I was exhausted. I had been fighting this for almost ten months. I was ready to give up.

Around 2AM, I heard someone say, "Wake up!" Then I felt a hand slide underneath my back and it sat me straight up. It was so quick that I was startled awake. My eyes shot open and I looked around. The light was on but there was no one in sight. I heard a voice say, "Open the closet." That didn't make sense to me because there was nothing in the closet. But I stood up and opened the door to Granny's bedroom closet. Inside the closet was a small, beige file cabinet. It had been left there by my aunt and uncle when they cleared out Granny's other file cabinets and her safe. They had looked inside and saw that there was nothing there. The voice told me to open that file cabinet. I knew the cabinet was empty because I had also looked inside before. There were only about 50 pieces of paper inside: photocopies of a flyer for a Mother's Day prayer breakfast. The voice said to take the papers out and look through them, one by one. Why on earth was I up looking at prayer breakfast flyers from five years ago at 2AM? I had no idea. Each page was a copy of the exact same flyer. And then suddenly, as I was flipping through the 70 pages of copies, I spotted one page that did not look like the others.

It was a receipt dated January 18, 1998. It was from an attorney.

The receipt ... had my name on it. It said for the creation of "a Will..... a Trust...and a Deed" and for "the petition for conservatorship in the estate of a minor." OMG! It had my name on it!

Granny DID HAVE A DEED!!! It had been 10 months since Granny passed away. I was brokenhearted, grief-stricken, nearly depressed, and had almost given up all hope. But late in the midnight hour, God showed up and showed out. I sent a screenshot of the receipt to my attorney who had helped with the family agreement. He suggested that I go to the courthouse and request the files for my estate case. My estate?! I didn't even know that I had an estate.

When I picked up the file from the courthouse, I couldn't believe my eyes! My grandmother's attorney had created a **pour-over will**[92], a trust and a deed to convey the property to the trust that she had created when I was 11 years old. Granny had signed and notarized all of the documents. She was after all, a businesswoman. It would have been quite unlike her to forget something as important as a deed.

The same year that Papa died, she had gone to court to ask the judge for permission to sell the house that was in my name. The judge had told her she could have permission to sell the house we owned in Detroit, if she established a trust that would transfer the condo to me when she died. The condo had been placed in a court-ordered trust and the trust was **irrevocable**[93].

I was ecstatic. This meant I no longer needed a family agreement or to open a Decedent's case in probate court to determine who had the rightful title to the condo. There was no question about it. I did! I was the rightful owner according to the 1997 trust (which was funded). Now, I could proceed with clearing the debt without worrying about her children coming after me to claim ownership of the condo.

Then again, was there even a debt to clear? Was the debt actually valid? Now that I knew the probate judge had ordered Granny to place the condo in a court-ordered trust, and the trust that her attorney created was irrevocable, could she have legally taken out a reverse mortgage? When I did a

title search on the condo, it did not show that Granny's trust deed had been recorded. However, if it had, the bank's reverse mortgage would have at best been second in line. I wondered, why had the deed had not been recorded. If the deed had been recorded, Granny would not have been able to take out a reverse mortgage.

Scratch a Lie, Find a Thief

I looked up my Granny's attorney, and, lo and behold, he was still alive. I found his number and set out to meet with him. I had made copies of the Probate court file, but if I were planning on recording the trust and deed with the Recorder of Deeds, I would need the originals.

When I met with Granny's attorney, he informed me that Granny's pastor had invited him to attend a meeting with he and her children at the church, on the week of her death. He also informed me that he had taken Granny's file with him to the meeting to discuss her estate. He claimed that when he pulled out her trust and deed, Granny's pastor informed everyone that she had a more recent trust from 2008 and that they wouldn't be needing the attorney's trust. However, Granny's attorney noted that the pastor had his secretary make a copy of Granny's will, deed and trust. According to Granny's attorney, the reason for the meeting was to help Granny's children figure out what to do about the insurance policy.

If you're saying, wait, Reese, what insurance policy? Then you're just as surprised as I was. But not to worry, you didn't skip a page. I now know why in the movie "Ray", Ray

Charles' mother's favorite saying was, "Scratch a lie, find a thief."

My grandmother's children had kept me completely in the dark about it, but Granny had taken out two term life insurance policies and named her trust as the **beneficiary**. When Bishop Elliot had met with Granny's children and me, they were just trying to see if I knew anything about the policies. Knowing that I didn't know about the life insurance policies gave them the green light to keep all the money without paying off the house. Once I scratched the lie —that my grandmother did not deed the condo to the trust — I found the people who were trying to hide the deed from me because it would reveal the 1997 trust, which instructed them to pay off the reverse mortgage with her insurance policies. As long as I didn't know about the insurance policies and the trust and deed, they could keep all of the insurance policy money for themselves. Thieves. But these weren't just regular thieves; I was the target of inheritance thieves.

Life Insurance Policies

Life insurance policies are great tools for passing on generational wealth. Why? Life insurance provides an income-tax free **death benefit**[94] that is immediately payable when the insured party dies. That death benefit is guaranteed for as long as the policy remains in force. The insurance proceeds can be for whatever the beneficiary wants (typically it's used to pay off debt, replace lost income, and allow those who depend on you to maintain their lifestyle.)

There are a handful of life insurance products, but the two most popular are term life and whole life. The other life insurance products combine death benefits and investing, such as universal life insurance, variable life, and other cash value policies.

Term life insurance[95] covers a person for 5, 15, 20, or 30 years. The goal of term life insurance is to replace your income if you pass away. If you die during the timeframe of the term, the policy pays out. If you die after the term expires, your beneficiaries get nothing. When you purchase a life insurance policy, you pay on it in the form of a **premium**[96]. The best bet is making sure that your policy has a **guaranteed level premium**[97] that won't change during your term (which usually comes with an upcharge).

What happens if you buy a traditional term life insurance policy and you outlive that term? Do you get a refund? No, not even a gold sticker. You will have to reapply for more term, or attempt to qualify for whole life. If you qualify, it typically requires a medical exam, and the cost of insuring you is much higher.

If you outlive your term and your policy is guaranteed renewable, you'll be able to renew term coverage. However, the new premium will be based on your age (and likely your health) at the time you renew, and it will be set based on your age, each year you renew it. So if you are 35 and take out a 20 year term and then live to 55 and want to renew, it will be much more expensive to renew at the rate of insurance for a 55 year old who may have had some health challenges. The rate will also possibly keep going up each year because of the risk involved with insuring someone older. Sometimes, an individual's health changes adversely to the point that they no longer qualify for the life insurance at all. This means all of those "low cost premiums" that they paid out over the term of their policy are a total waste.

On the other hand, a **whole life insurance**[98] policy (which is also called a **cash value** policy) does not have a term, you're covered for life. No matter what age you are when you die (up to 121 years old), your beneficiaries will be paid accordingly.

One of the important things to explore with a life insurance policy, in addition to the guarantees versus the projections, and whether the premium is locked in or flexible, is the type of **riders**[99] (add-ed on policy features) that are available. There are riders that will waive your premium if you become totally disabled, but will continue your coverage.

There is a rider called an **accelerated death benefit**[100] which means you can access the money in your policy in advance of your death, (for yourself rather than your beneficiaries). This rider will allow you to borrow against your death benefit if you become terminally ill (according to their set definition) and you can use the money you borrow as you see fit, whether it's to pay medical bills, cover household expenses or help pay someone to care for you.

I've heard a number of financial gurus, including Suze Orman and Dave Ramsey lament for hours about how term life insurance is the way to go and that whole life insurance is a rip off. According to those who are strictly pro-term life insurance, the reason they support term life is because it's a temporary product to fill a temporary void. After a certain period of time, you should not need it anymore, i.e. if you buy a 20 year policy and you have a 5 year old dependent, after the 20 year term and if you're still alive, your 25 year old will not need to replace your income with life insurance because they will have their own income to sustain them. According to Suze Orman, whole life policies cost about 5 times more than a term life policy and are overpriced.

For example, a 20 year level term life insurance policy for a 32 year old women would cost somewhere between $10 and $35 dollars a month.

Coverage Amount	Monthly Premium
$100,000	10.56
$250,000	$13.48
$500,000	$20.13
$1 Million	$34.04

If the insured passes away in that 20 year term, her family is guaranteed the coverage amount. But modern day medicine has advanced to the point that most people don't die from terminal illnesses immediately. Instead, they get sick and stay barely alive for 7-15 years depending on their illness. If a person is insured for a term and buys a 20 year $500,000 policy at age 32 and then gets diagnosed with cancer at 52, they are alive but the money they've spent would be gone and of no use to them. More importantly, being able to qualify for any insurance at this point is highly unlikely. The money they've spent on a term life insurance policy was less than $5,000 over 20 years, but they are now uncovered and **uninsurable**[101].

Money spent on term insurance: $20.13 x 12 months x 20 years = $4,831.20

Additionally, according to Dave Ramsey, cash value policies are bad because when the policyholder passes away, the **beneficiary**[102] never actually gets the cash value the policyholder paid extra for them to receive in addition to the **death benefit (face value)**. This is when the riders come into play to enhance the policy, which doesn't just benefit your loved ones, it also favors you as well. Many of the riders that you can add to a whole life policy can help you in your old age. One of the saddest things I've seen is my aunt who is 60 years old in poor health with relatively little assets not being able to stop working even when her health fails her because she doesn't have any security measures or policies in place to protect her.

If she had taken out a whole life policy and added an accelerated death benefit rider, it would pay her out $40,000 a year when she reached the age of 57, and things would look drastically different for her. She is a prime lesson in why you must learn to make your money work for you, rather than working for your money.

There's another concept of <u>Being Your Own Banker</u> taught by R. Nelson Nash in his book. He teaches people to use a life insurance policy to finance their life rather than the bank. It's pretty interesting and high level, so you'll want to spend some time researching it on your own. However, it seems to me that you'd need to have fairly large sums of money in this system for it to operate properly. Why? Because compound interest works best the more time or money you have.

The Magic Penny

Have you heard about the magic penny before? What about turning one little penny into over $10 million dollars? No?

Well before we on on to talk about this magical penny, let me ask you a simple question and I want you to answer it honestly.

Would you rather have $1 million dollars or one penny doubled every day for 31 days?

If I offered you $1 million right now or told you I'd give you a regular penny that will double every day for 31 days, which would you choose? I'm willing to bet dinner at a five star steakhouse that 98% of you are going to pick the million dollars. At first glance, it's quite tempting. If you operate in a poverty mentality, then I know for a fact you'd take the million and run. That sounds enticing, and who wants a penny that doubles? Well, check out why the regular penny might be a good choice!

The other 2% of you would pick the penny that doubled and I applaud you. Why? Because it's the right answer. You're thinking with a wealth-building mindset instead of the immediate gratification-centric poverty mindset. I used to be a part of the 98%, but I've since changed my thought processes ever since I read a book called <u>The Slight Edge</u> by Jeff Olson back in 2009.

Some of you are probably shaking your head thinking that a penny is worthless. I've actually seen a person sweep the floor and throw them in the garbage when he dumped the dustpan. Like most people, I hate getting and carrying around pennies, but if I can get one to double in value per day for 31 days, then I'd love me some pennies.

Allow me to let you in on a little secret as to how a penny can be so sexy. I'm going to show you the simple concept that has changed my mind about putting my money in a cash value policy. I'm going to show you what compound interest is all about. Some have called it the eighth wonder of the world. After learning the math behind it, I have come to the understanding that they're right. **Compound interest** is all that and then some!

If you could double one cent every day for one month, what would you get? You're probably thinking, "*A big mac!*" It's hard to comprehend this little equation. Want to guess what you would have if you doubled one cent every day for one month? Let me break it down…

Do you see that over there? Yes, you will get $5.3million when you take one cent and double it every day for 30 days. That's the real power of compounding interest. This is the same thing that powers investments and savings in general and that powers cash value life insurance policies.

Now, let me speak some truth first. This little math trick is to just show you the real power behind compound interest. You won't find any investment or savings account or cash value life insurance policies that provides you with 100%

returns. That would be unrealistic and you shouldn't expect it

Double a Penny a Day

Day	Dollars
1	$0.01
2	$0.02
3	$0.04
4	$0.08
5	$0.16
6	$0.32
7	$0.64
8	$1.28
9	$2.56
10	$5.12
11	$10.24
12	$20.48
13	$40.96
14	$81.92
15	$163.84
16	$327.68
17	$655.36
18	$1,310.72
19	$2,621.44
20	$5,242.88
21	$10,485.76
22	$20,971.52
23	$41,943.04
24	$83,886.08
25	$167,772.16
26	$335,544.32
27	$671,088.64
28	$1,342,177.28
29	$2,684,354.56
30	$5,368,709.12

to, because it just won't happen! Most investments,

particularly cash value life insurance have guarantees of close to 4% returns, but can fluctuate and go as high as 12%. Over the course of time, even 4% is a great deal of growth with the help of compound interest.

According to the life insurance companies, the upside to whole life insurance is that a portion of the premium is working to create an asset by building a cash value that you can borrow from. Yep, you can borrow from yourself. Thus, it seems that if you are only evaluating life insurance for the death benefit and the security that it will leave your children, then term is likely a better bang for your buck. However, if you are looking for a policy that can offer you benefits while you are alive, in addition to death benefits for not only your children but your grandchildren, whole life insurance appears to have more to offer you. Once you've grown a cash value, you can borrow against that cash value-tax free under certain conditions.

Although accessing the cash value via policy loans accrues interest and reduces the cash value and death benefit, if you structure it properly, you can use the loan option of the cash value whole life policy as a flexible source of funds. This loan also does not require a loan approval like a bank loan. In addition, it cannot be turned down like a bank loan. Loan amounts are only limited by the cash value balance, unlike a bank loan which must approve the loan amount. Also, the interest rate on a whole life policy loan is set and doesn't vary based on your credit score like a bank loan, and it can be paid back according to your schedule. Another plus is that a whole life insurance policy loan doesn't require a credit check.

How Much Life Insurance Do You Need?

Most financial advice books like those written by Suze Orman will tell you that the purpose of life insurance is to put your money to work, so that if you die, your loved ones won't have to suffer further crisis: meaning, if you're a wife and a mother of four and you get struck by lightning, life insurance would replace your income until your children were old enough to be able to live without your income. If your family currently spends $40,000 year and your youngest child is about 10, they would need $40,000 for approximately another 10 years, or $400,000. As the provider for your family, you have the ability to decide how well you want to provide for them in your absence. On a scale of one to five, with one being "begging on the street corner" and five being "living in the lap of luxury", most people would say that they want their immediate family to be as comfortable as humanly possible when they are gone. Therefore, they have the ability to choose a policy based on the premium they are willing to pay, which can determine if their family barely has enough to make it, or has enough to not work, stay in the house they currently live in, or move to a better house to keep the children in a comfortable environment.

A life insurance policy is one of the few ways in which a person can make provisions so that their family will never have to work again, even if they don't make much money. If you want them to be comfortable, instead of buying a $400,000 policy, you'd buy one that you expect would cover their annual expenses for the duration of their lives.

The goal is also to give heirs enough money so that if they invest the rest, they can live off of the interest and never have to actually spend the principal. If you take out a policy for $800,000, which is twenty times what your family spends a year, your family could invest the money. If they made only 5% a year off of their investments, they'd make $40,000, minus **capital gains taxes** [103], which covers their annual expenses. This is how to make your money work for your family. A death benefit of $800,000 seems like it would be very expensive, but a term policy purchased for a 30 year old, healthy person could cost as low as $30 a month.

It's this type of strategy that is often employed by knowledgeable families that changes the financial status of the entire family; however this type of wealth rarely gets passed along in Black families.

It wasn't surprising that my grandmother had taken out insurance policies. She was a very wise woman. And even more so, she didn't make the beneficiaries of the policies her children. She made the beneficiaries her trust, which she could change as needed. But since Granny had created a trust in 2008 and one in 1997, I needed to figure out which trust was the beneficiary of her policies.

Granny's pastor was listed as the **successor trustee**[104] for the court-ordered trust created by Granny's attorney in 1997. In 2008, Granny's health began to take a turn for the worst. While she was low on strength, her daughter had her create a new trust to try to steer control over Granny's assets to herself. Because my aunt lacked legal knowledge, the trust that she wrote was basically a carbon copy of the 1997 trust, with a few key changes. Although both documents stated that I was to inherit the condo, in the 2008 trust she removed the language which instructed the trust to pay Granny's "just debts with the trust funds." Instead the 2008 trust required the successor trustee to "preserve the trust property with trust funds." Although worded differently, both trusts gave their successor trustees the same instructions: to pay off the reverse mortgage with the insurance policies and preserve the condo.

Note: Unlike a will, trusts can't automatically cancel one another out just because one was created more recently than the other. A trust is a legal entity and it must be revoked by the **trustor** in the new trust to replace the old one, (unless the first trust is **irrevocable**). If the new trust does not explicitly revoke the old trust, or the first trust is revocable, then both can be valid. If either of them give conflicting instructions, they would need to be submitted to a Probate court. In Granny's case, she had two different trusts that controlled two different assets and they were funded separately; the 1997 trust controlled the condo, and the 2008 trust controlled her insurance policies, but the instructions in both were in agreement.

Since the insurance policies were controlled by the 2008 trust which was governed by my aunt, she would have free reign to do as she pleased as long as no one told me about the 1997 trust and the insurance policies. After going over the trust with Granny's attorney, he likely informed her that the 2008 trust (like the 1997 trust that he wrote) had a requirement that the trust funds be used to secure the trust property (the condo). Therefore, my aunt as the successor trustee of the 2008 trust would have had to use funds from the insurance policy to "secure" the condo by paying off the reverse mortgage. Paying off the reverse mortgage with the insurance policy funds would mean that I would receive a free and clear condo, and that she and her siblings would have to split whatever was left over, which at the time would have been $80,000, or $26,667 apiece. Why split $26,667 when you could just cut the grandkid out and double your share? Seemed like a good deal, and I'm sure it made great sense to all three of Granny's children.

After all, death can bring out the worst in people. In my family's instance, it turned my grandmother's children to characters from the Game of Thrones. They became treacherous— willing to lie, steal and cheat-- just to get their hands on $50,000. A poverty mentality can transform even the sweetest loved one to an unrecognizable spirit full of angst, envy, and black-heartedness. Had these same people used their rental properties to build more streams of income or invested their money in whole life insurance policies when they were my age, they would not be 60 and in dire need of Granny's money. I've watched these same relatives be wasteful with money, eating out five days a week and not being concerned with saving. I watched them live off of their mother by constantly calling on her to bail them out, and even pay their bills. They had lived off of her all their lives, and they were going to clamor for her last dime in death.

When I realized that Granny did have a trust and a deed, I reached out to her pastor and met with him. I informed him that I had found the 1997 trust and deed. He looked at me and said, "Who told you?" I said, excitedly, "Granny did from the grave." He looked away into the distance. Out of the blue, he stated, "Your mother wasn't part of it." Part of what? Why was he sticking up for her? I hadn't talked to my mother in over 6 months, but I knew that she and pastor still detested one another. Granny's pastor was basically admitting there was a whole ominous plan between my aunt, uncle, himself and Granny's attorney, but he wanted me to know that my mother wasn't involved. As unscrupulous as he was, even he didn't want to see money destroy a mother-daughter relationship.

Then he asked an even more insulting question "Have they gotten their money yet?"

"I don't know anything about anyone getting any money," I replied.

He sat back in his seat and said, "Well, if they got the money, it is long gone by now. What are you going to do? You can't get blood from a turnip."

Granny's Pastor, Bishop Elliot, had just acknowledged that he had helped to facilitate or was at least aware of a plan to commit **inheritance theft**[105]. Typically, inheritance theft strictly occurs as intrafamily violence, however, the pastor had legitimized the whole experience which made it possible based on my trust in him. Legally, he should have been held responsible for the **breach of fiduciary duty**[106]. After all, he was the one my grandmother named as successor trustee of the 1997 trust.

What did he do to breach his duty as successor trustee?

First, Bishop called a secret meeting with Granny's attorney to discuss her estate and failed to inform all of the beneficiaries. Second, he concealed the existence of the 1997 trust from its sole beneficiary. Third, he concealed the

$150,000 insurance policies, and lastly, he concealed the existence of the 1997 deed so that I could not take title of the property prior to it going to foreclosure.

    Naming a trust or executor of a trust or will is a very serious matter. Trustees and executors should be people that are impartial, unbiased, trustworthy, and licensed and bonded to handle the estates of others. Just because someone wears a clergy collar does not mean they should be trusted to transfer your wealth. The problem with having interested parties (ex-boyfriends, childhood friends, pastors) serve as trustee or executor is that they may take it upon themselves to re-allocate the assets of the decedent and redistribute them as they see fit. A trust can only protect those who know that it exists and know where to find it. However, trusts can be destroyed, hidden, or stolen. The reason sunset conversations are so important is because they put the heirs and beneficiaries on notice of what to expect and who to seek out when the time comes. If a person doesn't know who to designate to carry out their wishes, it may be best to retain an outside third party.

Chapter 8: *Investing in Your Future*

I have learned so many life lessons since Granny passed away in July of 2014, and all of this information came at me hard and fast. While facing a countdown clock, I frantically worked to save the condo from foreclosure while attempting to grieve. Although I was completely unprepared and unsuspecting that my own family members would try to disinherit me, I did everything that I could do to save the condo without holding them liable for their actions.

I attempted to save the property through the Michigan court system by requesting the court to hold the pastor, Bishop Elliot, and Granny's attorney, Mr. Morad, accountable for breaching their fiduciary duties. I also asked the probate court to provide a **constructive trust**[107] but it seemed that Bishop Elliot had used his megachurch connections to block my efforts. While personally battling four lawsuits in court, I realized that I had bitten off more than I could chew, and that adding four lawsuits on top of grief and unresolved family trauma was a terrible mix. I wasn't able to show up as the best version of myself because there was so much pain, frustration, confusion, anger, and heartbreak. I was already traumatized by the loss of the woman who raised me and the lawsuits were adding an unsafe amount of stress to a miserable situation. Some days I could barely get out of bed, and I would just spend the day sobbing in dismay at all that I'd lost. I felt like a part of me had died.

Once it became clear that the trial courts in Michigan were not willing to step in to correct the actions of Granny's attorney who failed to record the deed; or Granny's pastor who hid the existence of the trust and deed; and of Granny's children who hid the money from Granny's insurance policy that was instructed to first be used to pay off Granny's condo — it was very clear that if I wanted to keep Granny's home, I'd have to purchase it— rather than inheriting it free and clear, as my grandparents had intended me to.

If I were going to purchase the condo, it was no longer about my emotional connection to the property as I had to look at the purchase as an investment. Was purchasing the condo a good investment? I had to take off my emotional spender glasses with consumer lenses so as to see the world through **InvestHER lenses**.

When I called the bank's attorney and offered to buy the condo, I was told that the bank would have to perform a new **appraisal**. When Wells Fargo sent out the second appraiser, the price came back at $100,000. The 2-bedroom condo, which a mere four years ago was selling for $15,000, appraised for $70,000 two years ago, was now being quoted at $100,000! Impossible.

This changed everything. I had to erase all of my calculations and start over. I sat down to figure out if the property was still a good deal at $100,000. If I put down $1000 in **earnest money**, and borrowed $99,000 at a rate of 5% in 2017 via a **fixed rate 30-year mortgage**[108], the monthly payment would have been $531.45. Once taxes and **HOA fees** were included, the monthly expenses would have been $1353.45. Adding $350 in cost, utilities, upgrades, repairs and supplies would bring monthly costs to $1703.45 and would only leave a profit of $300 per month, on a good month.

Wearing my InvestHER lenses, this deal was beginning to look less and less attractive. The goal of every InvestHER B.A.B.E. is to maximize her **ROI** and get the largest amount of return possible. If I were going to borrow $100,000 at a 5% interest rate, I would need to be making at least 8% in returns to justify the **investment**[109]. $300 of profit per month was a little over 8% returns which was $266, but I wasn't convinced that the rental market would be steady in Detroit. And although I had made nearly $30,000 with AirBNB, I didn't want to risk it all by investing all of it back into the condo. It would have been too risky to put up my own savings, and have my AirBNB profits tied up in a condo in Michigan. I would have had nothing left in **liquid assets**[110], not even an emergency fund. If being house rich and cash poor was going to leave me without an "in case of emergency fund," then this was a "no deal"! InvestHER B.A.B.E.S. always cover our assets!

Investing Requires Strategy

Back in 2008, when Americans became acquainted with the term "Great Recession," the subprime mortgage bubble had burst, and banks were closing left and right. Property values slid into the toilet, the stock market was drowning, and the job market floundered. A great deal of people lost their homes because, without a job, they couldn't make their mortgage payments. I saw two bedroom condos in Granny's building for sale for only $15,000 because people couldn't afford a high mortgage and a high HOA combined. Because of the cyclical nature of the market, we can't expect that the recession was a one-time ordeal. In fact, all signs indicate that America may be due for another financial crisis, or at least bubble burst.

If the market is likely to auto-correct in the near future, we should be cautious about the amount of debt that we take on because we may be forced to unload it if the cost is too burdensome. When you buy things that you can't really afford, and your financial house isn't solid and secured, you can go belly up when the wind blows.

A large portion of a generational wealth portfolio is investments. Savings is very critical to have money available in case of emergencies and to use as a **down-payment**, however, when you have enough money to pay your bills and a cushy rainy day fund, the rest of your money should be actively working for you, recruiting its other dollar friends to come and join him. A big strategy of investment is to **diversify**[111] one's portfolio so that you are spreading your investments into different areas. Although buying a condo for $100,000 cash was feasible, it didn't strike me as a diversified investment strategy.

At the same time, after spending 3 years going to court and fighting blindly in the dark against things done behind closed doors and secrets from 15 years ago, I decided that I was investing too much of my life, my energy, my youth, and my happiness going back and forth to court trying to achieve justice when all I stood to gain was a two bedroom condo in blistery cold winter Michigan. I realized that the investment of my time and my health was worth more than the $100,000 condo that I was slowly starting to lose my health and joy over.

    I had to look at this from a different lens: my InvestHER lenses. If I had spent three years fighting in court, the most I could win was the right to the condo valued at $100,000, but if I spent three years working on a business or building my career, I could make over 3 times as much. So, I decided to work smarter, instead of harder. If I were going to save my time and energy, I needed to come up with the $100,000 to purchase the property outright. I decided to use my **leverage** to create an investment opportunity for people who lived outside of Michigan, and wanted to invest in real estate in Detroit. By leveraging my network, I solicited **OPM**[112] (other people's money). To explain the investment I put together a proposal that included the **cost-value analysis**[113] of the property, of the metro Detroit rental market, of the rising value of property in Michigan due to gentrification, of the cost of rehabbing the property, of the monthly fees and annual taxes, and the estimated cost of maintenance and supplies. I shopped the proposal to those I knew who were interested in investing in Michigan, and eventually, I came up with enough investors to purchase Granny's condo.

    I was no stranger to investing. I had made investments in the stock market since 2006. My stock picks had performed 26% above the market every year. Being an InvestHER B.A.B.E. was not like going to a casino, putting money in the machine and hoping to win. Investing required strategy. I tend to invest in the businesses that I know and love, and businesses that I can tell will be very valuable in the future based on looking at opportunities through my InvestHer lenses.

For example, back in 2014, my favorite rapper, Jay-Z, and his wife, Beyonce, announced that they were going on tour together. Tickets to sit in the *Good* seats were $500. Granny knew I was a huge fan and offered to buy the tickets for me. I almost accepted, but my wealth building mindset wouldn't let me allow her to spend $500 on a concert. But I knew many others would. The wheels in my mind got to turning. I wondered who the company was that would be putting on the concert, because it was sure to be sold out and very lucrative. I learned the company hosting the concert was Live Nation, that its stock was currently on the market at $21.18 per share. I decided to take $500 and instead, buy shares of Live Nation. Well, I was right, the concert was a hit, but more importantly, Live Nation puts on concerts all over the world, all the time, and they were a thriving business. As I'm writing this book, shares of Live Nation are now at $71.00 a share. My shares have tripled in value! Instead of paying Jay-Z and Beyonce $500 for a two hour show, Jay-Z and Queen B were making money for me! Now that's what I can a wealth-building mindset! Beyonce had indeed upgraded me.

Note: I am not an investment coach or a licensed financial adviser. I do not have a Series 7. This is not financial advice. I am a woman who invests regularly, and I'm speaking from my personal experience, which I'm sharing with you in order to help you understand the lay of the land; however my experiences may or may not be able to be duplicated in the market.

So, investHER B.A.B.E.S., let's talk about the basics of investing. I'll try to get through this the best I can without getting too much into the weeds.

An **investment** is where you commit your cash into a business, certain financial accounts, real estate, stocks, bonds, or other assets for the purpose of obtaining income and/or profit.

For those InvestHERs looking to put their money to work, the **financial markets**[114], often called the stock market or stock exchange, is an open forum where investors are allowed to trade stocks, bonds, and other financial assets. Financial markets are a pool of buyers seeking investments. The New York Stock Exchange is an example of a financial market (think grocery store of financial assets).

Bonds

Bonds[115] are a type of **lending investment** where you lend your money to an individual, bank, credit union, corporation, or government for a specific period of time. In return, you are promised interest payments and a return of your principal either **on demand** (whenever you want it), or at a specific **maturity date**.

Lending investments are usually low risk, and if you loan to a bank or credit union, the U.S. government insures your loan up to $100,000. **U.S. Treasury bonds**[116] are **coupon bonds** that are issued by the U.S. government. Treasury bonds cannot default as long as the U.S. Treasury can print money. For all other bonds, however, there is a risk of default. Bonds that mature in 2-3 years are short term and bonds that mature in 3-10 years are intermediate bonds, bonds longer than 10 years are long term bonds.

Bonds are traded in the financial market because you can't "cash in" a bond prior to the maturity date. The only way to get rid of it and get your money is to sell it in the market to another investor, thus, the price fluctuates. All bonds promise to return the principal (**face value** or **par value**[117]) back to you. Most bonds pay interest every six months. Each interest payment is called a **coupon**[118]. Treasury bonds pay fixed interest rates with coupons paid semiannually.

Corporate bonds[119] are the debts of corporations that companies issue to finance company costs. Unlike the Treasury bond, a company bond also add a **premium** to their yields so as to compensate investors for the **risk of default**[120]. Corporate bonds have a **rating**[121], (like a grade in school) which is a measure of how much they are at risk of defaulting. Companies like **Standard and Poor** (S&P), **Fitch**, and **Moody's** rate the credit-worthiness of the company which ranges from AAA to D. Anything above a B is considered low risk, or investment grade. Anything lower or without a grade at all, are called **junk bonds**. **Municipal bonds** are the debt of states and municipalities. Bonds can be purchased directly on the stock market or through a mutual fund, which pools a number of bonds together without charging brokerage commissions.

Stocks

Stocks[122] are **ownership investments** which allow investors to purchase a piece of ownership of a company. Ownership investments are typically more risky than lending investments, but have higher potential returns. For instance, if a company goes into bankruptcy liquidation, bondholders are prioritized to be paid from the company's liquidated assets before stockholders are. Individuals can invest in common stock by buying an ownership share on the stock market or through a stock broker, through a mutual fund, or directly from the company. Those who own stock, known as **shareholders**[123], have the right to vote for the board of directors who make decisions for the company. To make money from stocks, you can realize a **capital gain**[124] or the board of directors of the company can decide to pay stockholders **cash dividends**, a portion of the company's earned profits. Cash dividends can be paid on a regular basis, or as a one time payment.

Stocks are sold in a marketplace called the stock exchange, such as the New York Stock Exchange (**NYSE**), American Stock Exchange (**AMEX**), and National Association of Securities Dealers Automated Quotation (**NASDAQ**), which provides a standardized procedure for trading. The stocks enter the market when a company decides to **"go public"**[125] and convert from a **privately held company** to a **public corporation** whose stock is traded on an exchange and can be bought and sold by anyone. When stock is sold for the first time, it's called an **initial public offering**[126] or IPO. There are a number of tools for learning how to analyze individual stocks for possible investments, and those considerations are vast, but that is something too complex to be addressed here. *Note*: Part of becoming an investor is doing your **due diligence** to learn about the thousands of stocks that are traded each day, and the different strategies for evaluating them.

Once you've decided to purchase stocks, you will hold them in your **brokerage account**[127]. A brokerage account can hold your stocks electronically, such as Charles Schwab, Ameritrade, E*Trade, and their transaction costs and services vary. Most provide investment advice, stock recommendations, sell mutual funds, and help you to trade. Trading begins at 9:30 AM, and ends at 4:00 PM eastern standard Monday through Friday. Stocks are traded using a unique **ticker**[128] symbol of one to 5 letters. The price you're willing to pay in order to buy a stock is your **bid**, and the price you're willing to accept from someone buying stock from you is known as your **ask**. You can buy or sell in the open market at the best available price by placing a market order, or you can set the price that you want to pay with a limit order.

Mutual Funds

Mutual funds[129] pool and invest an individual's money into stocks or bonds as a substitute for directly purchasing stocks or bonds. When you own a mutual fund share, you indirectly own a small portion of a multi-million or multi-billion dollar portfolio. Mutual funds typically buy hundreds or thousands of different stocks, thereby providing much more diversification than you could buy on your own. Mutual funds also take the heavy lifting off the shoulders of the investor since they are carefully managed and selected by a team of professionals. Mutual funds can be purchased through brokerage firms, banks, or financial advisors. All mutual funds charge fees as a percent of your account balance (assets), and these **annual expense charged**[130] for managing the funds, vary. Mutual funds pay brokers, financial planners, and advisors a **sales load** for selling fund shares to investors. Some mutual funds are non-load. Some funds charge **transaction fees** for purchasing and selling shares to cover the cost of covering the transaction cost of buying and selling stocks in the fund portfolio.

Money market funds [131](MMFS) and **Exchange Traded Funds**[132] (ETFS) are specific types of mutual funds. MMFS pool the cash funds of shareholders and invest in money market securities, such as short term bonds issued by governments, government agencies and banks, and the shareholders make money from dividends. MMFS can be substituted for bank accounts, and typically pay higher yields than bank accounts and also allow investors to write checks and make withdrawals. MMFS are mostly used as a resting place for cash between selling a stock or mutual fund and buying another. An ETF is a **closed end fund** that tracks a specific stock index, and invests in the same companies contained in the index in direct proportion. So, for instance, the SPDR Standard and Poor's Depository Receipts track the S&P 500 index. ETFS typically pays dividends quarterly that closely matches the dividend yield of the underlying index, minus the annual fund expenses.

WHEW! That wasn't so painful, was it??? We have now had a crash course in the major components of investing 101.
Okay, well, get ready, we have just a bit further to go.

The other aspect of investing is for the purpose of **retirement**[133], which has three major types of vehicles: 401(k)s, traditional Individual Retirement Accounts (IRAs), and Roth IRAs. If used properly, retirement accounts provide huge tax savings in comparison to ordinary investment vehicles. Retirement investments attempt to look into the future to forecast your retirement needs, and allow you to maintain the standard of living that you desire by projecting how long your money will last you in a variety of future market conditions. You can't properly provide for generational wealth if your money doesn't stretch beyond your retirement. Unfortunately, if you aren't prepared to deal with inflation, taxes, and health care costs, then you won't have many assets to pass on to your heirs when you stop earning income.

401(k) plans[134] are employer based retirement plans that are defined by how much the employee contributes to the plan. (As opposed to pension, for instance, which is defined by the benefit the employee receives). Similar plans include **403(b)** and **457 plans** which are offered by schools, universities, and government employers.

One of the products that I find particularly beneficial for entrepreneurs building generational wealth is a **Solo 401k**. A **Solo 401k**[135] is a special type of 401k that is solely meant for self-employed individuals who do not employ any full time W-2 employees of their own. This plan has all the features of the more expensive plans, which includes an IRS-approved qualified plan status, a built-in Roth component, participant loan feature, maximum contribution limits, ability to invest into both traditional and alternative assets such as real estate, and direct **checkbook control** without the need for a custodian or an LLC. This plan which was created in 2001, allows single entrepreneurs to place up to $53,000 in the tax deferred account, and over $100,000 for married couples. Unlike most 401(k) plans which only allow for investments into stocks and bonds, a solo 401(k) plan is allowed to invest in alternative assets including real estate, private companies, and tax liens.

The more commonly known plans, **Individual retirement accounts**[136] (IRAs) are self funded and available to anyone with wage or salary income. Contributions to traditional IRAs are tax-deductible for low and moderate-income individuals. Contributions to Roth IRAs are not tax-deductible, but Roth IRA retirement withdrawals are tax free.

An employee's contribution to a 401(k) plan is not reported as income or subject to tax, however, when the money is withdrawn, income taxes have to be paid on them. By not paying taxes on the money until withdrawal, you're able to earn a return on the government's income tax money for decades. Many employers will also match employee contributions in 401(k)s. Taking advantage of these matching programs could produce a substantial increase in your retirement wealth. However, some employers require you to work a certain number of years before their contributions **vest**. Typically, a company will offer their stock in addition to mutual funds to invest in as part of the 401(k) plan. If you leave the company, you can keep the money in the plan, roll it over into another employer's plan, or transfer it into an IRA.

Everyone with $5,500 of employment income is allowed to contribute to a **traditional IRA**. However, taxpayers must make less than a certain amount in order to contribute to a **Roth IRA**. The traditional IRA and a Roth IRA differ in one fundamental way, Roth IRA contributions are not tax-deductible, unlike with traditional IRAs and once money is held inside a Roth IRA for 5 years and the investor has reached 59 1/2, the withdrawals are not taxed at all, but traditional withdrawals are taxable. The ability to avoid all income taxes on the investment returns in a Roth IRA is a huge advantage for many investors, particularly those who expect their tax rate to be the same or higher in retirement. You can't take loans against IRAs, unlike a 401(k), and you can't withdraw the money prior to the age of 59 1/2 without penalties.

Investing for retirement is intended to be less risky so that when you reach retirement, you are likely to have saved enough money to carry you through old age. However, younger people, particularly millennials who were caught in the Great Recession, may be well served by taking on a few more risks with some of their investments. One of the hottest trends right now in investing is cryptocurrency, and many are flocking to figure out if they can make fortunes there.

Cryptocurrency

Cryptocurrency[137] is a form of digital currency that lets you make online payments to other people or businesses without having to go through a third-party, like a bank. Records of these transactions are stored in a sequence of data blocks called a **blockchain**, which is stored and duplicated on thousands of computers around the world; this is how the system remains relatively accountable and transparent.

Currently, there are about 1,500 types of cryptocurrency, including **Bitcoin, Ethereum, Ripple**, and **Litecoin**. You can buy the "coins" in a variety of ways, including paying cash for them on an exchange like **Coinbase** and **CashApp**, providing goods or services in exchange for the currency, or purchasing them from a **Bitcoin ATM**. After you've bought cryptocurrency, you store them in an **"online wallet"** or on an external hard drive, **cold storage**.

Initial Coin Offerings (ICOs) involves an investor purchasing cryptocurrency coins that aren't part of a registered offering, but one that provides the promise of a future stake in a startup venture. In these cases, the startups create their own "coins" to sell to investors.

Cryptocurrency sounds like it is super high-tech, but digital currency has actually been around for years in one form or another. Loyalty programs like airline frequent flyer miles, hotel points, and credit card points are all forms of digital currency. The benefits you receive from these programs are not in dollars, but in the company's self-created currency. So, this is something a lot of us are familiar with already.

Some people have made really good money investing in cryptocurrency, present company included. However, one must be careful with such an undertaking. When Bitcoin was launched in 2010, the price of one coin was $0.01. That same coin December of 2017, was worth around $20,000. The value of Bitcoin rose more than 1,000% in 2017 alone. With those kinds of returns, you'd actually think that we'd all want to get in on the game, right? But by August of 2018, a single Bitcoin was back down to $6,000. Which brings me to one of the things I want to stress most: cryptocurrency has been extremely volatile.

Warren Buffet, the CEO of Berkshire Hathaway and a highly respected investment guru, has said that he won't touch Bitcoin. He believes that its dramatic rise and fall has been driven mostly by supply and demand, and not because the currency has any **inherent value**. In other words, he views cryptocurrency as speculation, and not an investment.

The distinction is very important to understand. Investing involves taking a calculated risk in order to achieve an expected return based on the price and quality of what something's worth today. **Speculating**, on the other hand, means buying something regardless of its value—in an attempt to make a profit by later selling it to someone else for a higher price.

Trading in cryptocurrency is largely **unregulated**. The coins are not backed by a government or a central bank, like the U.S. dollar is. And the **U.S. Securities and Exchange Commission** doesn't oversee the buying and selling of this kind of currency.

In addition, even though cryptocurrencies have been designed to be theft-proof because of the blockchain sequence, there's also a chance of fraud and cybercrime. For example, in June of 2011, the Japan-based Mt. Gox (which was then the largest Bitcoin exchange) experienced a security breach in which $450 million worth of Bitcoin was stolen. In December of 2017, the Slovenian cryptocurrency exchange, NiceHash, was hacked for a loss of $64 million.

In the case of ICOs, there's substantially less investor protection than in traditional securities markets with more opportunities for fraud and manipulation, and fewer protections for investors in the event of theft.

Additionally, Bitcoin has a much more simple risk called human error. You need a login ID and password to access cryptocurrency exchanges. If you forget those—or they're lost or stolen in a hacker or phishing scam—you can lose your access, and your currency. Unfortunately with no issuing or regulating country or authority for cryptocurrencies, there's very little recourse in cases of fraud or theft. And law enforcement often has limited ability to seize it.

Thus, cryptocurrency comes with a number or risks; however, if you believe in the phrase "no risk, no reward," and you have an appetite for a challenge, then you might be open to a more risky money move. My rule is to only spend money that you can afford to lose. Let's say you have $200 that's been allocated in your budget for clothes, shoes, hair and makeup, and you decide to forgo spending on those items for three months. Instead you decide to use that $600 for a risky cryptocurrency investment. That is $600 that you were comfortable parting with. If the entire $600 goes up in a cloud of smoke, you haven't put your future in jeopardy.

For those who are completely risk averse, more stable investment options exist including **commodities** like beef, corn, natural gas and **tangibles** like gold and silver. Many believe that purchasing gold and silver in the form of bullion or coins, are a sure way to protect themselves in the event that the market completely crashes, inflation skyrockets, or the whole financial system falls apart. They also believe that during this time the only functional currency will be gold, silver and diamonds and other tangible limited resources. During periods of past market stress, investors have often turned to gold as a perceived safe haven asset. Gold is the one asset that has literally survived time. Gold is impervious to air and water, meaning that every ounce that has been mined in history still resides somewhere on earth.

This belief was supported by a famous actress back in the day named Zha Zha Gabor, who said that when her family had to flee to Hungary during Nazi occupation, they sewed their jewelry into the linings of their coats, so that they could later use them to barter for food, shelter, or clothes. Surely, there is wisdom embedded in this kind of advice, particularly with the current climate being as polarized as it is.

Gold and silver coins can be purchased from online retailers, but not the U.S. government. Prior to 1933, the U.S. dollar was backed by gold reserves held by the government, and the dollar had a **gold standard**, which meant that you could exchange $20.67 for an ounce of gold. However, when the government removed gold as the backing for U.S. currency, many began storing up gold reserves on their own. I personally believe that it is very useful to have a few pieces of gold and silver around as a type of "insurance policy".

Now that you understand the basics, allow me to share a few InvestHER B.A.B.E.S. tips that I learned from my grandparents that have served me well.

InvestHER B.A.B.E.S Guidelines

1) **Only spend what you can afford to lose.** Don't invest with your bill money, unless you're ok being homeless. If you can buy it with cash, do so. If you need to leverage your credit, do it short term. Why pay interest you don't have to?

2) **Research new opportunities, and talk to everyone**, from the janitor to the CEO, because you never know what you'll learn from whom.

3) **When you hit a lick, go all in.** When my grandparents found a way to get houses from the city of Detroit through the tax sales, they purchased close to 20 rental properties. They took advantage of the opportunity with full force.

4) **Diversify your portfolio.** If you invest in real estate, try both commercial and residential; if you invest in risky stock, also invest in something stable like bonds.

5) **Invest for the good times and the bad.** Have you ever wondered who makes money during bad times? If the market crashes, what stock goes up the most? Look to have investments for when the market is thriving and when it is sinking. The market is cyclical, but trouble don't last always.

6) **Put yourself back on the gold standard.** My grandparents believed that having a diversified portfolio wasn't complete without tangibles like gold and silver coins.

7) **"When I had the funds to fund the game, this hand wasn't never slow. I'm out of funds ya know."** When you have spent more than you can afford, get out of the game. It's far better to buy what you can afford, than to rent what you can't.

8) **Read to learn. Invest in information.** My grandfather was a voracious reader and had books on everything from "How to Buy Stocks" to "How to Win Friends and Influence People."

9) **Always stay ten steps ahead.** My grandfather was a master chess wizard and knew that the game of chess was a metaphor for the game of life. To win, you must stay ahead of your opponent. "Stay ready so you don't have to get ready."

Chapter 9: EntrepreneuHERship

Since Granny had passed, I had grown tremendously as a woman, as an investHER, and as a Believer, but that growth came at a price. I learned about trusts and insurance policies as a result of being the target of inheritance theft. I saw firsthand what having a poverty mindset can drive family members to do. I learned about estates, probate, and successor trustees and what happens when someone breaches their fiduciary duty. I learned that I was stronger than I thought, and that God truly had my back even in the darkest valley. But also, I got the chance to learn who Granny was, not as a matriarch, but as a businesswoman.

Granny's life was one of the best examples of being a prudent investHER. She invested her time, talents and treasures in order to create a life that looked much different from the humble beginnings where she came from. Granny invested in herself and her family, in love and marriage, in learning and entrepreneurship, in community service and charity, in traveling and culture, in her church and her ministry. With such widespread investments, it's no wonder that her life was worth writing about.

As I was cleaning out her home after she passed away, I found a newspaper article written in 1968 interviewing her about her career choice. Granny explained that as a mother of three, she couldn't spend 8 years going to college, so she decided to learn computer technology instead. By learning a cutting-edge skill, she invested in herself, and it turned out to be a very profitable move.

In this present day and age, everything we do is with a computer. We not only have computers in our homes, but we also have them in our phones and even in our watches. It's almost impossible to go a full day without using a computer in some capacity, but back in the 1960's, computers were relatively new. They were so expensive that only large companies and the government could afford to have them. They were so huge that they filled up a whole room. Worst of all, no one knew how to use them.

It took great wisdom back in the 60's to look at such an intimidating machine and say, I'm going to learn how to use it! But, that's exactly what Granny did. She taught herself how to use the computer, after having been a typist for the army. Later she taught herself how to use computers to book travel. She was able to get high paying jobs and make great money working for different companies like American Airlines and Federal Mogul.

As a seasoned professional in the travel industry, Granny used her contacts to explore places she had always heard of like Hong Kong, the Fiji Islands, and Israel. Her love for exploring the world allowed her to open up the minds of those around her. Granny invited family and friends on her journeys. She took people who had previously never stepped foot outside Detroit around the world on exotic expeditions.

After being one of the first people who learned to use the computer in order to make travel reservations, she decided to open her own travel agency in 1977. Later, she purchased the entire block of commercial property where her travel agency was located and opened more businesses in them, which she ran for over 20 years. When I asked Granny why she opened a travel agency, she said that Papa had gotten tired of her having multiple side hustles and wanted her to focus on one business and put all her effort in it. As a result, Granny's travel agency served some of the biggest named pastors and gospel artists in the world. She worked with the likes of CeCe Winans to Pastor Noel Jones. Over time, her celebrity clients became her close friends and invited her to travel with them to red carpet events like the GRAMMYs. And of course, I was right there by her side.

Choosing to harness her time, talents, and treasure turned Granny into a millionaire with a jet-setter lifestyle and a few top gospel artists as her personal friends. My blessing was being able to tag along with her to Seoul, where she had us fitted for clothes made by a tailor, to Acapulco where we luxuriated in villas with private swimming pools, and to Hollywood where we conversed at Grammy award receptions. My grandmother was able to give me the gift of exposure to life beyond Detroit, and as a result she caused me to want to flourish, and build a legacy that I can share with my own future granddaughters.

The Bible says "Who can find a virtuous woman?" After my grandmother passed away, I realized that I had indeed been raised by one. Verse 16 of chapter 31 says, "She considereth a field, and buyeth it: with the fruit of her hands, she planteth a vineyard." My modern day translation of that scripture is, "She is a savvy real estate investor, and reinvests her profits to build a business on top of the land she acquired." How amazing is that? My grandmother fulfilled the description of a virtuous woman to the letter!

Proverbs 31:10-31 King James Version (KJV)	A Virtuous Woman: B.A.B.E.S.' Edition
10 Who can find a virtuous woman? for her price is far above rubies.	Have you ever seen anyone like her? She's one of a kind. Simply priceless.
11 The heart of her husband doth safely trust in her, so that he shall have no need of spoil.	Her husband has full faith and confidence in her, and his life will always be better because of her.
12 She will do him good and not evil all the days of her life.	She will treat him well, and not inflict pain.
13 She seeketh wool, and flax, and worketh willingly with her hands.	She takes care of business at home. She makes sure to keep her home impeccable.
14 She is like the merchants' ships; she bringeth her food from afar.	She buys organic, non-GMO foods, to provide the best nutrition for her family.
15 She riseth also while it is yet night, and giveth meat to her household, and a portion to her maidens.	She gets up before sunrise to provide breakfast for her family and instruction for her house staff.
16 She considereth a field, and buyeth it: with the fruit of her hands she planteth a vineyard.	She is a savvy real estate investor, and reinvests her profits to build businesses on top of the land she acquires.
17 She girdeth her loins with strength, and strengtheneth her arms.	She builds her core with strength training, and her arms are toned.
18 She perceiveth that her merchandise is good: her candle goeth not out by night.	Because she is business savvy, her investments do well and her investments make money while she sleeps.
19 She layeth her hands to the spindle, and her hands hold the distaff.	She works to create the best image for her family by making sure they always have clean, well kept clothes.
20 She stretcheth out her hand to the poor; yea, she reacheth forth her hands to the needy.	She is charitable and works to uplift others.
21 She is not afraid of the snow for her household: for all her household are clothed with scarlet.	She always thinks ahead, no matter what the season. She has already made provisions so that her family is ready to take on the day.
22 She maketh herself coverings of tapestry; her clothing is silk and purple.	She decorates her home and herself with the most luxurious fabrics and the most opulent style. Everything about her is plush.
23 Her husband is known in the gates, when he sitteth among the elders of the land.	Because she is honorable, men of greater status and wealth give props to her husband.
24 She maketh fine linen, and selleth it; and delivereth girdles unto the merchant.	She uses her gifts to have multiple streams of income and even a side hustle. Money is always coming to her from somewhere.

25 Strength and honour are her clothing; and she shall rejoice in time to come.	Her business acumen and her brand's goodwill, will continue to open doors for her in the future and will make her wealthy.
26 She openeth her mouth with wisdom; and in her tongue is the law of kindness.	When she speaks her words are wise, and when she gives instruction its delivered with kindness.
27 She looketh well to the ways of her household, and eateth not the bread of idleness.	She manages her household like a well run corporation, rather than sitting around watching reality tv shows, while her house is in shambles.
28 Her children arise up, and call her blessed; her husband also, and he praiseth her.	Her husband and children are proud of her and husband is always showing her off to the world.
29 Many daughters have done virtuously, but thou excellest them all.	Many women operate in excellence, but she exceeds them all.
30 Favour is deceitful, and beauty is vain: but a woman that feareth the Lord, she shall be praised.	Finessing eventually gets exposed, and being a baddie gets old, but a woman who walks in the power of God will always be worth her weight in gold.
31 Give her of the fruit of her hands; and let her own works praise her in the gates.	Put some respect on her name and give credit where credit is due, shower her with accolades, honorary degrees and titles because she deserves those too.

A wise man once said that, "A mind, once stretched by an idea, never returns to its original dimensions." The same is true for a mind that has been exposed to a wealth-building mentality. When you begin to operate with a wealth-building mentality, you'll begin to see each decision to spend money as an opportunity to invest or to consume. Because the decision-making process requires such a detailed analysis, you'll find it almost impossible to turn off, and you'll start to apply that criteria for every decisions. A wealth-building mindset slowly permeates every area of your mind.

Becoming an investor in real estate and in financial markets, will, over time, build a muscle in you that looks at the world not as a consumer (which is a poverty mindset), but as an entrepreneuHER and investHER. As you build your ability to see your money as a resource that can be invested to build greater wealth, you will also learn the value of your time and your talents.

Time, talents, and treasures are the three gifts that are deposited in us all to build generational wealth. The more you use your money with wisdom and discretion, the more you'll want to also use your time and talents with precision and decisiveness.

Intentionally choosing to use your time and talents for building your own generational wealth will lead you to walk the path of an **entrepreneuHER** because every step of what you focus on will be to build yourself. When a B.A.B.E. is an employee, she works to gain and build skills, sharpening tools, and creating contacts that will serve her when she eventually becomes an entrepreneuHER. Even if an entrepreneuHER is employed, she will never approach her work with an employee mindset. For more details, see Chapter 1 of <u>The B.A.B.E.'S Guide to Winning in the Workplace</u>.

Being an entrepreneuHER requires a wealth-building mindset. The B.A.B.E.S.' Guide series were written to support and celebrate every beautiful, ambitious, brilliant, entrepreneuHER. The B.A.B.E.S. Foundation champions entrepreneurship as a core trait of our audience identity because we believe that when we speak to entrepreneuHERs, we are speaking to a very specific type of woman. We believe that entrepreneuHERial women are built with a different fiber; they have a streak of boldness, they have a healthy dose of confidence, they are risk takers, they are big-picture thinkers, and they want the best for themselves and are unwilling to take 'no' for an answer.

Every B.A.B.E., at some point in her life, will start a business to make money because she believes that she can offer a product or a service that people will pay her for. Having the courage to take an idea, apply effort and energy to turn it into a tangible product or service, and then having the confidence to offer that product or service to the world means that you're one incredible B.A.B.E. We entrepreneuHER B.A.B.E.S. who take such risks, bet the house on ourselves, and are willing to believe in the possibilities for which there is no current manifestation of.

B.A.B.E.S. are capable of calling their visions into existence by sheer willpower. That ability to believe in yourself is the most powerful tool an entrepreneuHER can ever possess. An entrepreneuHER who dares to believe in the power of her dreams, will always have a mode of transportation to take her from her present reality to manifesting everything she has ever hoped for.

Unlike employees who trade hours working for money, entrepreneuHERs think more broadly about income. Those with a poverty mindset believe that opportunity is scarce, thus, they strive to have a job that will provide them with security through paychecks, pensions and employee benefits.

However, those with a wealth-building mindset don't trade time for money, nor do they find safety in employment, they seek out risk and live well off the rewards. Wealthy people and people with a wealth-building mindset don't work for money. They work for **equity** (ownership rights). Rather than working for other people, they work with other people to achieve their financial goals.

In one of the songs released by The Carters, Beyonce says, "Pay me in equity, watch me reverse out of debt." What Beyonce knows is that when you partner with others who have a wealth-building mentality and are skilled at building profitable companies, choosing to receive ownership rights in their company that will vest at some future date, rather than just being compensated with present value cash, can be far more lucrative.

These partnerships allow investHERs to make far more money in the future than they would if they were paid today. Delaying gratification with spending is similar to the delayed gratification with entrepreneuHERship; and, with both, you're choosing to recoup the benefits later. By working and building your own business structure or system, investing in creating a product or service, then marketing it, you are willing to earn less now in order to rake in so much more later.

A person who only trades hours for wages is limited in how much money they can make. The cap is typically set by their employer. However, a person who works for themselves is only limited by their own ability and knowledge. Thus, they have no ceiling because as long as they continue learning and expanding their mind and capacity, their potential for growth is unlimited.

Therefore, the cost of entrepreneuHERship is a simple formula, Risk + Time + Talent. Risk, being the willingness to take a risk on yourself. Time, being the time needed to learn how best to capitalize from your product/service. And Talent, being the work it takes to build the vision from concept to reality. For any B.A.B.E. interested in succeeding as an entrepreneuHER, there is a learning curve and she must first be willing to spend the necessary time learning what she doesn't know.

She also must be willing to put in the work of building her vision from a concept inside her mind to a tangible finished product or service that people can purchase. The risk will be the willingness to spend her time, talent, and treasure on creating something that didn't exist before, and being willing to bet on her ability to create, while sacrificing other opportunities. Everything has a cost, and entrepreneuHERship typically requires great sacrifice.

The photos that entrepreneuHERs post on their social media describing how much they make, their celebrity clientele, or how quickly their business is growing is a result of weeks, months, and years of foundation laying, information gathering and strategy building. EntrepreneuHERs often pay someone to coach them or consult with them on how to build their business, and those services rarely come cheap. Also the amount of time one has to spend away from their family and friends is another cost of doing business, particularly in the startup phase.

Being an entrepreneuHER will require preparation--planning, prayer, precision, and positioning. Once you have a God-given idea or you recognize that your God-given gifts are profitable, your job is to put in the work so as to bring that vision to fruition. One of my favorite stories in the Bible is of the boss with three employees found in Matthews 25:14-29. Allow me to re-tell it the way I read it: the boss was traveling and would be away on a business trip for a while, so she gave her three employees investments. She gave the first employee five investments, she gave the second employee two investments, and the third employee one investment.

When she returned after being gone for a long time, she called all her employees. She asked the first employee what she'd done with the investment, the employee revealed that she'd invested the five investments and made another five. The boss was proud and rewarded her employee. The boss asked the second employee what she had done. She said that she'd invested the two investments and made another two. The boss was proud and rewarded the second employee. The boss asked the third employee what she'd done with the one, she said that she knew that the boss would be upset if she lost it, so she put them away and didn't touch them. The boss called her lazy and took her talents away and gave it to the employee with ten talents.

The lesson learned was that for those who have much, more will be given to them, but for those who have little, the little they have will be taken away from them. This story clearly illustrates how each of us has the responsibility to use the gifts and talents that God has given us, and work with them until they produce even greater returns.

The story in Matthew also reveals another lesson: when the employee with one talent hid the talent by burying it, her boss ridiculed her by calling her lazy and saying that she should have taken the talents to the bankers (exchangers) and invested it with them so that when her boss returned, she would have made interest off of the investment. The lesson here isn't that she didn't put in enough sweat equity, it was that her thought process was incorrect.

Her mindset was evil because she had a poverty mentality rather than a wealth-building mentality. The first two employees had a wealth-building mentality and knew to invest because it would return a profit over a period of time. Knowing how to skillfully invest talents, time, and treasures is a matter of working smarter. Taking the money to the bankers and putting it in a high interest account isn't particularly difficult to do, but you have to know how interest compounds over a period of time. You also need to know how to compare the present value of money to the future value of money so as to know why it makes sense.

The truth is that the third employee was not lazy or wicked, she was fearful. She was afraid of losing the money. So, rather than using it to invest and potentially losing it all, she decided to put it up and hide it. In Matthew 25: 25, she said "And I was afraid, and went and hid thy talent in the earth..." Hiding talents is the same as hiding your God-given gifts and God-given ideas. The reason the boss called the third employee lazy and wicked is because her mindset focused on scarcity rather than abundance. One of the greatest threats to an entrepreneuHER is fear— the fear of inadequacy. If an entrepreneuHER has a poverty mentality, or focuses on scarcity, they can easily be tricked to believe that they are not enough, or that their business product or service is not valuable. That mindset can hold an entrepreneuHER hostage and paralyzed in her productivity. Many women have a great deal of self-doubt that manifests as fear, and that doubt causes self-sabotage when doing business. Even I, at a point in my life, have felt inadequate and attempted to shrink away from my purpose. Believing that you aren't good enough or that your product isn't going to sell is what holds most entrepreneuHERs and aspiring entrepreneuHERs back from greatness.

In order to overcome that fear, we must conquer our blind spots. Have you ever heard that phrase, "You don't know what you don't know?" Well, it's true and in this digital day and age, information is abundant. Learning what you don't know can happen in a matter of minutes by picking up your phone and saying, "Hey Siri, what is…?" or standing in your living room and saying, "Alexa, what is…?" However, when it comes to business, we can't be lazy; we just have to put on our pumps and go to wherever the information that we need is— whether that means asking for a meeting with someone whom you'd like to mentor you, attending a conference where specialized information is shared, or going to the point person on a contract and asking for help. The key to being successful is knowing what you don't know and making sure you minimize your blind spots. With an abundance of information in circulation, you can't afford not to know. It's your duty to have the right information that creates a slight edge for you above and beyond your competition.

EntrepreneuHERship isn't just about what you know, it's about the knowledge possessed by the team you surround yourself with: everyone from your social media intern to your HR person must continue to learn to be at the top of her game. The business of running a business requires that you have a few key players: 1) corporate attorney, 2) accountant 3) tax consultant 4) marketing/ PR strategist and 5) tech person.

Without these core team players, having a business will be rather difficult because you'll be forced to wear multiple hats, and won't be able to focus on what you do best and oversee the entire operation.

The benefits of entrepreneuHERship are as vast as you can imagine. One of the top benefits of building a business is that you can pass it on to your children during your lifetime, or leave it to them in your death. My grandmother had built a successful, world renowned travel agency with a strong customer base, as well as a popular full service beauty salon, and a boutique that sold the cute hats, furs, and clothes that she purchased during her travels. As she and her husband got up in age, she wanted to turn the business over to her children. Unfortunately, her children were not interested in carrying on the business, so she had to close it.

Being an entrepreneuHER is fantastic for the purpose of having freedom, but there may come a day when you no longer want to work in the day-to-day operations of the business, a day where your health changes, a day where your familial obligations are calling, or a day where you simply decide that you want to retire. For a B.A.B.E., having an exit strategy in mind is critical to being an entrepreneuHER because she must know what her end goal looks like when she starts on her journey. For my grandmother, her end goal was to create a successful business that she could run while spending time with her family, allowing her to make her own hours, see the world, enjoy time with her friends while making money, and create a way to give back to her community. Granny's travel agency did all of that and more. Unfortunately, because her children didn't share her understanding of investing nor appreciate her wealth-building mindset, they were only interested in enjoying the benefits of the travel agency, rather than doing what was necessary to keep it going. When the travel agency closed, Granny became a full time caretaker of her ailing mother and husband. Her businesses had provided her with enough income to move on comfortably and care for those whom she loved the most.

The downside of entrepreneuHERship is that when you stop working, your business stops working. Thus, it's advisable that if you are an entrepreneuHER, you should seek to build a system that operates the business while you are away or become an investHER in the business of others so that your money can work for you, while you bankroll other entrepreneuHERs whose businesses you deem to be solid investments. This is the next level of being in business, and with the right information, mentorship, and coaching, you can learn to build thriving platforms or a portfolio of companies that you've invested in. When you build a system, you're able to leave that to your children or grandchildren to run if anything ever happens to you. In this regard, you've passed on two of the most critical components of generational wealth — freedom and self-determination.

Chapter 10: *Your True Inheritance*

Hey guys, we've made it! The home stretch, the last chapter, the grand finale. And since you've stuck it out with me for this long, I'm going to let you in on a secret that I've learned and only few will understand. You will receive many gifts over the course of your life. If someone who treasures you **bequeaths**[138] you a gift that has a dollar value, you are very fortunate. It is truly a kind gesture to think enough of someone to leave them some of your earthly possessions after you've transitioned. My grandmother bequeathed me her heart-shaped necklace, which I never take off, because it reminds me of her and makes me feel like she's watching over me everywhere I go.

However, those who love you the most will bestow gifts to you that are more valuable than all the diamond necklaces at Tiffany & Co. The most valuable inheritance is worth more than money can buy, including knowledge and wisdom, compassion and kindness, diligence and self-worth, drive and confidence, self-determination, and spiritual discernment. These gifts together will serve you more than anything you could buy at a store. These gifts are your true inheritance. So, no need to fear inheritance theft because your true inheritance isn't intangible and can't be stolen.

When I was in college, the pastor of the church I attended, Dr. Stacia Pierce, had a saying, "success leaves clues." The clues of success are the type of characteristics that money can't buy and school can't teach. If someone has amassed a fortune, you can learn from them how to do the same. This is a perfect example of why people with a wealth-building mindset who've hit a roadblock (or even if they hit rock bottom) will still rebound. Since they know HOW to build wealth, no one can ever take that knowledge away from them. Thus, they will soon be back on top, even if they currently have 50 cents to their name. If you ask the right questions, you too can use their lessons to guide your journey to success. The key is to learn from people who have built wealth: what their lessons were, what their trials were, and how they have recovered. Even if I had not inherited property from my grandmother, the tools of how to write a book and the tools of how to manage business well, all stemmed from things I'd learned from her.

(The only thing I wasn't able to learn before she passed was how to choose a husband, but we'll talk more about that in the next book, stay tuned).

Going through Granny's papers after she passed away allowed me the opportunity to see the 76 years of life that she lived in black and white. In her business transactions, in her bank statements, in her real estate purchase documents, in her letters of recommendation, and in her mortgage payoff documents, Granny was a B.A.B.E. about her business. Being able to sort through her papers after she passed wasn't a chore at all, it was a gift. In sorting through her papers, I was finding the one last gift she left for me, "how to build wealth and how to build a beautiful life." Granny had left me a blueprint.

When I had left the hospital in 2014 after she took her final breathe, I was devastated, broken-hearted and I felt like I was all alone in the world. The one person who had loved me unconditionally had stopped breathing and I had nowhere to go that I could call home. Sure! I had a fully furnished apartment in DC with nice furniture, but I was homeless because home is where the heart is and my heart had died. I came back to Granny's condo and fell to pieces. I crumpled up like a discarded love poem balled up in a corner. I sobbed, "Granny, I'm homeless." But in my spirit I heard her speak to me. Her voice said, "Now it's your turn, I have taught you how to build a home, you have everything you need: love. Now it's your turn."

And with that, for the first time in my life, I realized that I was ready to be a homeowner. I was ready to build a thriving successful business, invest in real estate, residential and commercial property, invest in timeshares for our annual family getaways, invest in stocks and bonds, have bountiful brokerage accounts and million dollar insurance policies, invest in gold coins and other tangibles, and lastly, to invest in my church and my community. This was my blueprint that I've shared with you. I have the same power to build, just as Granny did, and you do too.

While I thought I needed to inherit Granny's place, I battled for three years in court trying to secure the transfer of it because it was the only place that gave me the feeling of home, the truth is that I have everything I needed to build a new home, and even multiple homes around the globe. I have multi-million dollar condos waiting for me. All I have to do is walk in my gift and purpose.

Even more so, when I stopped battling for what I knew was mine, God began to show me that, "The battle is not yours, it's the Lord's". After I had done all that I knew how to do by filing lawsuits to stop the foreclosure, to holding Granny's attorney accountable, to holding Granny's pastor and successor trustee accountable, and to asking the probate judge to hold himself accountable, I had not been successful in my efforts.

I lifted my hands and surrendered to whatever it was that God had for me. I wasn't going to keep fighting for years to save what had been wrongfully taken from me. I was willing to let God give me the desires of my heart. "Casting all your care upon him; for He careth for you." 1 Peter 5: 7. I decided to "Be anxious for nothing, but in everything, by prayer and petition, with thanksgiving present your requests to God." Philippians 4:6.

What I learned in the process (that Granny probably tried to teach me at some earlier point in my life, but it didn't register) was that sometimes God tells you to roll a boulder up a hill, not because He actually expects you to move the boulder, but because by you approaching the boulder daily, by planting your feet in the ground and summoning all your strength in your shoulders, quads, and calves to push the boulder, you get stronger every time. Although the boulder is too big for you to move, sometimes God just presents a test to see if you'll push with all your might, just to test your obedience. But in true God-like fashion, He loves to show off in your life once you lift your hands and surrender.

I'm a witness! So, all of the fighting, trying to push a boulder up a hill, and trying to understand what happened almost 20 years prior with my estate was just so that I could see what happened if I fought with all of my might versus what He could do. Just when I thought that I had lost it all, God showed up and showed out, talk about #RestorationSeason! God surprised me and gave me the desires of my heart. Not only to become a homeowner, but to also be an investor in rental property.

"And I will give thee the treasures of darkness, and hidden riches of secret places, that thou mayest know that I, the LORD, which call *thee* by thy name, *am* the God of Israel." Isaiah 45:3

Following in my grandparent's footsteps is an incredible feeling. Following the blueprint that they left for success with all of the tools that they left me is a gift that I thank God for on a daily basis. This gift was so powerful that I had to share it with you. In the course of this book, you might have been reading and saying to yourself, "Well, Reese that's easy for you to say. You had wealthy grandparents. You're a Black trust fund baby, but I wasn't so fortunate." That may be the truth about your past, but it won't be the truth about your future. As the saying goes, "If you don't come from a wealthy family, then a wealthy family has to come from you!"

Because I've shared Granny and Papa's wealth building mindset and wealth building tools, the onus is now on you to build a better future for the next generation of your family. When I say my morning confession, one of the sentences goes

"Wealth is my birthright and my reality." Speak life into your finances and into the finances of your family.

Children and Money

And as you start building your life and future, think about the legacy that you'll leave for you children. When you give gifts to children you care about, perhaps consider instead of giving them a toy, provide them with financial gifts that can literally keep on giving returns in the form of stocks, bonds, savings accounts, wealth building books, and even real estate.

When my friends and relatives give birth to a new baby, I gift them with shares of stock. In order to gift investment assets to a minor, you must first establish a **custodial brokerage account**[139] on her or his behalf. There are two types of custodial accounts: a **Uniform Gift to Minors Act (UGMA)** or **Uniform Transfers to Minors Act (UTMA)**. The two account types are largely the same, though contributions to UGMA accounts are limited to cash, insurance policies, and securities such as stocks, bonds or mutual funds, whereas, you can contribute virtually any kind of asset to a UTMA account, including real estate. The availability of the two account types and the age that the beneficiary may take control varies.

Contributions to both account types are considered **irrevocable,** because they belong to the beneficiary and cannot be reclaimed. Gifting a child with stock can actually teach them about the rise and fall of the market. It's important to start this lesson very early in life. I remember babysitting my cousin when she was only two years old. I turned to her and said, "Hey babycakes, what stock do you want me to buy you?" She said clear as day, "A-A-E" pronouncing each letter clearly. I thought it was funny, but something told me to go online and search for what she had said. I looked it up and lo and behold, AAEH was a real stock. I decided to take the two year old's advice and buy her 100 shares. Within a year it doubled. When a savvy little investHER B.A.B.E. speaks, I listen!

Another gift idea is a **College Savings Accounts**[140]. A college savings account can help children and grandchildren to successfully graduate from college with a lower debt burden. A **529 college savings plan** provides federal tax-free growth and tax-free withdrawal for qualified expenses, like tuition. **Coverdell Education Savings Accounts** are another federal tax free growth and tax-free withdrawal account for qualified expenses like tuition, school supplies, and room and board. To be eligible for these accounts, your **adjusted gross income** must be less than $110,000 or $220,000 for married couples, and contributions are limited to $2,000 per child.

My grandparents also purchased **savings bonds**[141] for me when I was a child. Savings bonds are a great way to show children how money grows over a period of time. An **EE bond** earns a fixed rate of interest for up to 30 years. An **I Bond** earns a fixed rate of interest plus an additional inflation adjusted rate, which can protect young investors if inflation rises. Gains made on savings bonds are tax exempt when used for college expenses.

Also, when dealing with children, it's very important that you help them build their entrepreneurial muscles early.

Teach them how to earn money based on a niche. Show them how to find a need. When I was about 12 years old, my grandmother was part of an auxiliary at a church called the Comforter's Ministry. The Comforter's Ministry had nothing to do with bedding; instead, we were like human binkie blankets. The Comforter's Ministry would show up to comfort a member of the church if a loved one had died. They would bring a greeting card, food, and come by the house to help with the grieving process. In short, they spread the love of God, and uplifted the downtrodden.

I would go with my grandmother to visit grieving families, and when we arrived, I would hand them a greeting card. One day, Granny stopped at the dollar store to stock up on more greeting cards. I realized that she was buying 50 to 75 cards for $1.00 each. In my mind, I calculated that the average cost of the cards were $75. I had just gotten my first computer and printer, and I decided that I could go home and print out greeting cards on card stock for the cost of an ink cartridge and a pack of heavy paper and pocket the rest.

I priced out a color cartridge and a new pack of paper, then I went home and designed my first greeting card. I even created my own branding, "Reese's Grphx", complete with a logo. The back of the card said "This card was printed exclusively for the Comforter's Ministry by Reese's Grphx." I had marketing y'all!!! My grandmother thought that the cards were great quality, so she set up a meeting where I could ask the Director of the Comforter's Ministry, Mr. Patterson, if I could be his exclusive card supplier. He loved the idea and placed an order for 150 cards, at $150 dollars. I had just closed my first major business deal. I was ballin y'all!!!!

This experience taught me that whenever I see a need, I can create a solution and charge money for it. These kind of lessons are invaluable and will encourage the children in your family to have a wealth-building mentality, rather a poverty mentality. They will be able to spot an opportunity anywhere they find themselves.

Granny took me to the church credit union and showed me how to place my money in my savings account. Although I could barely see over the counter, I still felt like a big girl. A simple savings account is the gateway to teaching kids critical financial lessons-- from wealth accumulation to the power of compound interest. Helping them compare statements from month to month can be its own lesson in financial literacy.

In addition to buying gifts, it's important to buy books that teach young people how to build wealth. Some of my favorite authors include Dr. Boyce Watkins, Suze Orman, and Gail Perry-Mason. All of these people were critical to growing my financial literacy. Gail Perry Mason even has a camp that people from all over the world send their kids to participate in, called the "Money Matters for Youth Camp," which teaches young people how to be investors, and even takes them to Omaha, Nebraska to the shareholder's meeting with Warren Buffet and Berkshire Hathaway.

The days of waiting to teach children about money are long gone. The earlier you start, the better for you and your children, even if it's making children come up with a service that they can provide, setting their price, and having them pitch it to you. The muscle of wealth building can form very early, and with your help, your children will be able to say that their family helped them prepare to build generational wealth.

"Beloved, I wish above all things that you may prosper and be in health, even as your soul prospers." 3 John 1:2

Today, I wish that for you and all your generations to come, continued prosperity and great health, even as your soul prospers. Generational wealth is yours if you're willing to claim it. B.A.B.E.S., Let's get to work!

I want to hear from you!

Thank you for reading my book. What did you think about it? If you enjoyed it, won't you please take a moment to leave me a review at your favorite retailer? Your feedback is so helpful!

To send your suggestions, comments, questions, encouragement, or for bookings and speaking engagements, contact me below:

M. Reese Everson, Esq.

Email:MRE@MReeseEverson.com

Be a Part of the Movement!

Check out our website:
www.MReeseEverson.com

Follow us on Twitter:
@TheBABESGuide

Follow us on Instagram:
@TheBABESGuide

LIke us on Facebook:
www.Facebook.com/TheBABESGuide

Glossary: B.A.B.E.S.' Wealth-cabulary

[1] An **inheritance** is the gift of honor and support given by a patriarch to his sons and sometimes daughters. It was meant for provision and to preserve the status of the family.

[2] **Wealth** is a large amount of money or valuable possessions. I define wealth as substantial assets that a person accumulates, typically built from income.

[3] An **asset** is something valuable that an entity owns, benefits from, or has use of, in generating income.

[4] **Appreciation**, in general terms, is an increase in the value of an **asset** over time. The increase can occur for a number of reasons, including increased demand or weakening supply, or as a result of changes in inflation or interest rates. This is the opposite of depreciation, which is a decrease over time.

[5] **Red-lining** is a lending practice which refused loans specifically to Blacks with the excuse that it was due to them living in an area deemed to be a poor financial risk.

[6] **Generational wealth** the passing down of valuable assets that one worked to acquire to someone younger in their family tree.

[7] (source: http://heller.brandeis.edu/news/items/releases/2018/meschede-taylor-college-attainment-racial-wealth-gap.html)

[8] An **heir**, is any person that is entitled to receive a share of the deceased's (the person who died) property.

[9] An **inheritance** is the practice of passing on property, titles, debts, rights, and obligations upon the death of an individual.

[10] A **testamentary** document is used to document someone's last wishes, typically a will or a trust.

[11] A **will** is a legal document that a person creates in order to give instructions on how they want their valuable possessions to be distributed after they die. A will has to be evaluated by a judge so as to see if it is legal and valid.

[12] A **trust** is a legal entity that a person creates for the sole purpose of giving instructions on how they are distributing their valuable possessions when they die. The trust does not need to be evaluated by a judge, and if it is properly set up it can operate as an independent legal entity that acts on your behalf when you die.

[13] When a person dies **intestate** the person who passed away does not have a will or trust.

[14] The **jurisdiction** is the location where something legally has rights to control or govern.

[15] A **deed** is a legal contract for the transfer of real estate which lists all the details of the transaction including who currently owns the property (**grantor**), who the future owners of the property are (**grantees**), how much value is being given in exchange for the property (**consideration**), the legal description of the property, and the date when the transfer is completed.

[16] A **grantor** is a person that transfers rights in a property from themselves to another party.

[17] A **grantee** is a party who receives the rights in a property from another party to themselves.

[18] **Consideration** is how much value is being given in exchange for the property that is being conveyed.

[19] When you get a document **notarized** you have it certified by a person authorized to authenticate that your signature belongs to you. The usually put a stamp and a seal next to your signature.

[20] A **Quitclaim Deed** is a document that transfers the rights of the current owner to a new owner.

[21] **Recording** a deed is when you take the deed to the Register of Deeds that it can be legally and publicly documented.

[22] The **Register of Deeds** or the **Recorder of Deeds** is an office that keeps a public list of all the property that had been bought, sold, transferred.

[23] An **Executor** is the person listed in the will who is to be legally responsible for the carrying out the instructions in a will, on behalf of the deceased (testator).

[24] A **Life Estate** is created when the property owner holds on to part of the rights to the property that they've legally transferred to someone else, for themselves

[25] When something **vests** it means the person has an absolute right some present or future interest in something of value. When a right has vested, the person is legally entitled to what has been promised and may seek relief in court if the benefit is not given.

[26] **Tenancy** is the right to live in a property for the rest of a set period of time, even if that period of time is unknown, such as "for the rest of their natural life."

[27] A contract that is **void** is not valid and cannot be legally enforced. Contracts with children or those who are mentally incompetent are usually void.

[28] A **lady bird deed is** a special form of life estate deed that gives the owner continued control over the property until his or her death. Once the owner dies, the property is transferred automatically to the new owner without the need for probate

[29] A **petition** is a request for legal intervention from a Probate Court.

[30] **Probate Court** handles matters dealing with the affairs of a minor or handicap person

[31] An **estate** is the total property that is owned by anyone including their assets and liabilities.

[32] A **Petition for Appointment or Conservatorship** is a request to be appointed the person legally responsible and accountable to the court, for the financial affairs of a third party.

[33] A **Protective Order** is a Probate Court order that permits the Conservator to take a specific action regarding the property that belongs to the minor.

[34] A **Guardian ad litem** is an attorney the court appoints to investigate what solutions would be in the "best interests of a child."

[35] An **irrevocable** document can not be later changed.

[36] A **funded** trust is one which has property transferred to it. In order to fund a trust with real property, you must transfer the property to the trust via a deed.

[37] **Malpractice** is negligence or misconduct of a professional person, like a lawyer who fails to meet the standard of care that is required by the profession, and the client is injured or damaged because of their error.

[38] A **sunset conversation** takes place when a person who strongly believes that they are at the sunset of their life, decides to share directions and information with an heir on how to carry out their wishes.

[39] (Source: https://www.forbes.com/sites/camilomaldonado/2018/07/24/price-of-college-increasing-almost-8-times-faster-than-wages/#20e46cb066c1)

[40] A **PLUS Loan** is a student loan offered to parents of students enrolled at least half time, or graduate and professional students, at participating and eligible post-secondary institutions.

[41] (Source: http://www.collegecalc.org/colleges/michigan/michigan-state-university/)

[42] U.S. Government-backed **student loans** were first offered in the 1950's under the National Defense Education Act (NDEA), and were only available to select categories of students, such as those studying engineering, science, or education degrees. The first federal student loans, however, were direct loans capitalized with U.S. Treasury funds. When Congress wanted to expand that, student loans were extended more broadly in the 1960's under the Higher Education Act with the goal of encouraging greater social mobility and equality of opportunity. The federal government began guaranteeing student loans provided by banks and non-profit lenders in 1965. After forty-five years, government guaranteed loans were eliminated in 2010 through the Student Aid and Fiscal Responsibility Act, and replaced with direct loans because guaranteed loans benefited private student loan companies at taxpayer's expense, but did not reduce costs for students.

[43] **Subsidized federal student loans** are only offered to students with a demonstrated financial need. Financial need may vary from school to school. For these loans, the federal government makes interest payments while the student is in college. For example, those who borrow $10,000 during college owe $10,000 upon graduation.

[44] **Unsubsidized federal student loans** while being guaranteed by the U.S. Government, does not include government payment on the interest for the student, rather the interest starts accruing during college. Nearly all students are eligible for these loans regardless of demonstrated need. Those who borrow $10,000 during college days owe $10,000 plus interest upon graduation. The **accrued** interest is further **capitalized** into the loan amount, and the borrower begins making payments on the accumulated total.

[45] Something **subsidized** has partial financial support from public funds.

[46] **Interest** a charge for the use of credit or borrowed money.

[47] **Principal** is the original amount of a debt on which interest is calculated.

[48] (Source: https://www.forbes.com/sites/camilomaldonado/2018/07/24/price-of-college-increasing-almost-8-times-faster-than-wages/#20e46cb066c1)

[49] (source: Edmiston, Brooks, and Shelpelwich 2013)

[50] A **rainy day/emergency fund** is a stash of money equal to at least three months worth of all expenses and bills.

[51] **Affordable Housing Programs** are usually tax rebate incentives provided to apartment building developers for setting aside of a set number of rental units to be made available at less than the going market rate, based on the income of the resident.

[52] **Passive Income** is any money that you don't have to trade time continually to make.

[53] **Charitable Contributions** are funds given to a charity or nonprofit organization. Typically the organization is a 501(c)(3) or some form of tax-exempt entity.

[54] A **poverty mentality** is a lack of financial literacy coupled with poor spending habits, poor saving habits, and little to no investing. Those with a poverty mentality operate in the spirit of lack.

[55] A **reverse mortgage** is a loan that allows a borrower to borrow a fraction of the value of their home, in exchange for the bank having the right to foreclose on the home when the die.

⁵⁶ A **loan** is a transaction whereby property is lent or given to another on condition of return or, where the loan is of money, repayment.

⁵⁷ A **predatory loan** is the practice in which a loan is made to a borrower in the hope or expectation that the borrower will default.

⁵⁸ A **Home Equity Conversion Mortgages (HECM)** is a reverse mortgage sponsored by the **United States Department of Housing and Urban Development (HUD)** which allows a senior citizen to take a loan out borrowing against a fraction of the equity in their home in exchange for the bank having the right to foreclose on the loan when the borrower default. The borrower is considered in default when they die or move from the home.

⁵⁹ The **United States Department of Housing and Urban Development (HUD)** is a government agency which insures HECMs. HUD's mission is to provide quality, affordable homes for all. The housing HUD insures and funds must be decent, safe, sanitary, and in good repair.

⁶⁰ A **lump sum payment** is an amount of money you receive all at once rather than in increments over a period of time.

⁶¹ A **line of credit** is an agreement between a bank and an individual to provide a certain amount in loans on demand from the borrower. The borrower is under no obligation to actually take out a loan at any particular time, but may take part of the funds at any time.

⁶² **Collateral** is assets with monetary value, such as stock, bonds, or real estate, which are pledged as security for a loan.

⁶³ **Default** is the failure to make payments of interest and principal on a debt.

⁶⁴ A **foreclosure** is the legal process by which a lender acquires possession of the property securing a mortgage loan when the borrower defaults.

⁶⁵ An **eviction** the legal process of throwing a resident out of a home.

⁶⁶ The **market value** is a subjective estimate of what a willing buyer would pay a willing seller for an asset, assuming both have a reasonable knowledge of the asset's worth.

[67] A person who dies without a will or trust is said to have died **intestate**.

[68] A **Decedant's estate** is a case opened in the probate court in the person's home state to determines who has the right to inherit the person's assets. The process, known as administration, can be time consuming and expensive, and the outcome may or may not reflect what the intestate person would have wanted.

[69] A **Personal representative** is a legal representative who manages the affairs of another.

[70] An **heirs state** means that when a person dies intestate (without a will or trust governing one or more of their assets) the heirs automatically inherits the asset.

[71] A **deed in lieu of foreclosure** is a deed instrument in which a mortgagor (i.e. the borrower) conveys all interest in a real property to the mortgagee (i.e. the lender) to satisfy a loan that is in default and avoid foreclosure proceedings.

[72] A **mortgage** is a loan for the purchase of real property, secured by a lien on the property.

[73] **Conspicuous consumption** is the purchase or display of expensive items to attract attention to one's wealth or to suggest that one is wealthy.

[74] **Depreciation** is when something reduces or declines in value or price.

[75] An **auto lease** is a contract granting use of a vehicle during a specified period in exchange for a specified payment.

[76] **Homeowner Association (HOA) fees** is an amount of money that must be paid monthly by owners of certain types of residential properties, and HOAs collect these fees to assist with maintaining and improving properties in the association, including maintenance, repairs and security of common areas.

[77] The **cost of living** is the average cost of the basic necessities of life, such as food, shelter, and clothing.

[78] (Source: American Millennials have less money than other generations did at their age -- but studies show an alarming amount of them have delusional ideas about their wealth)

[79] A **title search** or **property title search** is the process of retrieving documents evidencing events in the history of a piece of real estate, to determine relevant interests in and regulations concerning that property.

[80] **Earnest money deposit** is a deposit paid to demonstrate commitment and to bind a contract, with the remainder due at a particular time.

[81] A **closing** is the final transaction between a buyer and seller of real property. At the closing, all agreements between buyer and seller are finalized, documents are signed and exchanged, money passes to the seller, and title to the property passes to the buyer.

[82] The **Truth in Lending statement** informs the borrower of all the costs involved in applying for and closing a loan. Your statement should include how much is being financed, the cost of borrowing the money (finance charge), the annual percentage rate APR, the number of payments, the amount of payments, and the total that will be paid in principal and interest over the life of the loan.

[83] The **Good Faith Estimate of Closing Costs (GFE)** is a list of fees involved in providing the mortgage loan. It includes lenders fees, the cost for the appraisal, credit report, flood determination, recording and title fees as well as an estimate for homeowners insurance, taxes, prepaid interest, and mortgage insurance.

[84] **Return on Investment (ROI)** is a performance measure used to evaluate the efficiency of an investment or compare the efficiency of a number of different investments. ROI tries to directly measure the amount of return on a particular investment, relative to the investment's cost.

[85] A **turnkey** property is residential real estate that, upon purchase, can be rented out immediately by the buyer.

[86] An **FHA insured loan** is a US Federal Housing Administration mortgage insurance backed mortgage loan which is provided by an FHA-approved lender. FHA insured loans are a type of federal assistance and have historically allowed lower income Americans to borrow money for the purchase of a home that they would not otherwise be able to afford. To obtain mortgage insurance from the Federal Housing Administration, an upfront mortgage insurance premium (UFMIP) equal to 1.75 percent of the base loan amount at closing is required, and is normally financed into the total loan amount by the lender and paid to FHA on the borrower's behalf. There is also a monthly mortgage insurance premium (MIP) which varies based on the amortization term and loan-to-value ratio.

[87] A **down payment** is an initial amount given as partial payment at the time of purchase.

[88] The **Multiple Gross of Rent** is the amount of money that you can charge for all the units combined.

[89] **Cash Flow-Positive** means your cash inflows exceed your cash outflows.

[90] To **refinance** debt the borrower borrows additional money, thus creating a second debt in order to pay the first.

[91] A **short sale** is a sale of real estate in which the proceeds from selling the property is less than the amount owed.

[92] A **pour over will** is a will of a person who has already executed a trust. A pour over will is a protection which is intended to guarantee that any assets which somehow were not included in the trust become assets of the trust upon the party's death.

[93] When something is **irrevocable** it is unable to be canceled or recalled; that which is unalterable or irreversible.

[94] A **death benefit** is insurance money payable to a deceased person's stipulated beneficiary.

[95] **Term Life insurance** is life insurance that provides coverage at a fixed rate of payments for a limited period of time, the relevant term. After that period expires, coverage at the previous rate of premiums is no longer guaranteed and the client must either forgo coverage or potentially obtain further coverage with different payments or conditions. If the life insured dies during the term, the death benefit will be paid to the beneficiary.

[96] A **premium** is a sum of money paid for insurance.

[97] A **guaranteed level premium** is when a premium is guaranteed to be the same for a given period of years.

[98] **Whole life insurance (cash value policy)** is insurance on the life of the insured for a fixed amount at a definite premium that is paid each year in the same amount during the entire lifetime of the insured.

[99] **Riders** provides an additional benefit over what is described in the basic insurance policy, in exchange for a fee payable to the insurer.

[100] **Accelerated death benefit rider** is a benefit that can be attached to a life insurance policy that enables the policyholder to receive cash advances against the death benefit in the case of being diagnosed with a terminal illness.

[101] **Uninsurable** means a life insurance customer does not qualify for life insurance usually due to either a too risky profession, a disease diagnosis or a history of severe health problems such as stroke, cancer, diabetes or heart surgery.

[102] A **beneficiary** is the recipient of funds, property, or other benefits, from an insurance policy or trust.

[103] **Capital Gains Tax** a tax that is triggered only when an asset is sold, or "realized."

[104] A **successor trustee** is a person appointed if a trustee resigns or dies, who holds the title to the property in the trust.

[105] **Inheritance theft** occurs when a person, such as a caregiver, friend, neighbor, new spouse or advisor uses his or her relationship with a testator to obtain or take money or property from the testator that the testator intended to leave to his children or other legal heirs that are the natural objects of his affection.

[106] A **Breach of fiduciary duty** happens when the fiduciary acts in the interest of themselves, rather than the best interest of a party they have a duty to.

[107] A **constructive trust** a trust created by a court (regardless of the intent of the parties) to benefit a party that has been wrongfully deprived of its rights.

[108] A **fixed rate 30-year mortgage** is a long-term loan that you use to finance a real estate purchase, typically a home. Your borrowing costs and monthly payments remain the same for the term of the loan, no matter what happens to market interest rates.

[109] An **investment** is where you commit your cash into a business, bank account, real estate, stocks, bonds, or other asset for the purpose of obtaining income and/or profit.

[110] **Liquid assets** are those assets which are held in the form of cash, or assets which can be quickly converted into cash.

[111] To **diversify** is to purchase different types of securities in different companies in unrelated industries.

[112] **OPM** stands for "other people's money" which means using borrowed funds to purchase property rather than paying all cash.

[113] The **cost-value analysis** is a decision-making tool used to determine the feasibility of a project or investment, or the probability of its success.

[114] The **financial market,** often called the stock market, is an open forum where investors are allowed to trade stocks, bonds, and other financial assets. Financial markets are a pool of buyers seeking investments. The New York Stock Exchange is an example of a financial market.

[115] A **bond** is a **lending investment** where you lend your money to an individual, bank, credit union, corporation or government for a specific period of time. In return, you are promised interest payments and a return of your principal either **on demand** (whenever you want it), or at a specific **maturity date**.

[116] **U.S. Treasury Bonds** are debt obligations of the US Treasury that have maturities of more than 10 years.

[117] **Par value / face value** is the minimum price at which a share of common stock is initially issued to investors.

[118] A **coupon** is each interest payment paid on a bond.

[119] **Corporate bonds** are the debts of corporations that companies issue to finance company costs.

[120] **Risk of default** is the chance that companies will be unable to make the required repayments to their bondholders.

[121] A **rating** is a measure of how much a corporate bond is at risk of defaulting.

[122] **Stocks** are **ownership investments** which allow investors to purchase a piece of ownership of a company.

[123] **Shareholders** are those who own stock.

[124] A **capital gain** results when you buy stock and sell them for more than what you paid.

[125] **Going public** is when a company converts from a **privately held company** to a **public corporation** whose stock is traded on an exchange and can be bought and sold by anyone.

[126] An **initial public offering** or IPO is when stock is sold for the first time.

[127] A **brokerage account** holds your stocks electronically, such as Charles Schwab, and their costs and services vary.

[128] A **ticker** is a unique symbol of one to 5 letters used to trade stocks on the exchange market.

[129] **Mutual funds** pool and invest an individual's money into stocks or bonds as a substitute for directly purchasing stocks or bonds.

[130] **Annual expense charges** are fees charge as a percent of your account balance (assets) by all mutual funds for managing the funds.

[131] **Money Market Funds MMFS** pool the cash funds of shareholders and invest in money market securities, such as short term bonds issued by governments, government agencies and banks, and the shareholders make money from dividends.

[132] An **ETF** is a **closed end fund** that tracks a specific stock index, and invests in the same companies contained in the index in direct proportions.

[133] **Retirement** is withdrawal from one's occupation or position, especially upon reaching a certain age.

[134] **401(k) plans** are employer based retirement plans that is defined by how much the employee contributes to the plan.

[135] A **Solo 401k** is a special type of 401k that is solely meant for self-employed individuals who do not employ any full time W-2 employees of their own.

[136] **Individual retirement accounts** (IRAs) are self funded and available to anyone with wage or salary income. Contributions to traditional IRAs are tax-deductible for low and moderate-income individuals. Contributions to Roth-IRAs are not tax-deductible, but Roth-IRA retirement withdrawals are tax free.

[137] **Cryptocurrency** is a form of digital currency that lets you make online payments to other people or businesses without having to go through a third-party, like a bank.

[138] To **bequeath** someone is to leave a gift of personal property to someone, usually via a will.

[139] A **custodial brokerage account** is an irrevocable account that holds the contributions of stocks, mutual funds and other investments for a minor.

[140] A **college savings account** is a tax free growth account that can be used for qualified expenses like tuition.

[141] A **savings bond** is a tax exempt bond with a fixed rate of interest that can be used to help with college expenses.

Made in the USA
Columbia, SC
20 May 2020